Small Trees

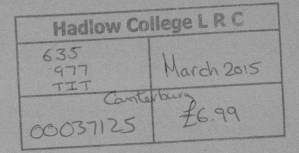

Alan **Titchmarsh**
how to garden

Small Trees

BBC
BOOKS

10 9 8 7 6 5 4 3 2 1

Published in 2012 by BBC Books, an imprint of
Ebury Publishing, a Random House Group Company

The Random House Group Limited Reg. No. 954009

Addresses for companies within the Random House
Group can be found at www.randomhouse.co.uk

FSC
www.fsc.org
MIX
Paper from
responsible sources
FSC™ C004592

The Random House Group Limited
supports the Forest Stewardship
Council® (FSC®), the leading
international forest certification
organisation. All our titles that are
printed on Greenpeace approved
FSC® certified paper carry the
FSC® logo. Our paper procurement
policy can be found at www.
rbooks.co.uk/environment

A CIP catalogue record for this book is available from
the British Library.

ISBN 978 1 84 990220 5

Produced by OutHouse!
Shalbourne, Marlborough, Wiltshire SN8 3QJ

BBC BOOKS
COMMISSIONING EDITOR: Lorna Russell
PROJECT EDITOR: Caroline McArthur
PRODUCTION: Rebecca Jones

OUTHOUSE!
COMMISSIONING EDITOR: Sue Gordon
SERIES EDITOR: Polly Boyd
SERIES ART DIRECTOR: Robin Whitecross
CONTRIBUTING EDITOR: Julia Cady
EDITORS: Sue Gordon, Anna Kruger
DESIGNER: Louise Turpin
ILLUSTRATIONS by Julia Cady, Lizzie Harper, Susan Hillier,
Janet Tanner
PHOTOGRAPHS by Jonathan Buckley except where
credited otherwise on page 96
CONCEPT DEVELOPMENT & SERIES DESIGN:
Elizabeth Mallard-Shaw, Sharon Cluett

Colour origination by Altaimage, London
Printed and bound by Firmengruppe APPL,
Wemding, Germany

Contents

Introduction

Gardening is one of the best and most fulfilling activities on earth, but it can sometimes seem complicated and confusing. The answers to problems can usually be found in books, but big fat gardening books can be rather daunting. Where do you start? How can you find just the information you want without wading through lots of stuff that is not appropriate to your particular problem? Well, a good index is helpful, but sometimes a smaller book devoted to one particular subject fits the bill better – especially if it is reasonably priced and if you have a small garden where you might not be able to fit in everything suggested in a larger volume.

The *How to Garden* books aim to fill that gap – even if sometimes it may be only a small one. They are clearly set out and written, I hope, in a straightforward, easy-to-understand style. I don't see any point in making gardening complicated, when much of it is based on common sense and observation. (All the key techniques are explained and illustrated, and I've included plenty of tips and tricks of the trade.)

There are suggestions on the best plants and the best varieties to grow in particular situations and for a particular effect. I've tried to keep the information crisp and to the point so that you can find what you need quickly and easily and then put your new-found knowledge into practice. Don't worry if you're not familiar with the Latin names of plants. They are there to make sure you can find the plant as it will be labelled in the nursery or garden centre, but where appropriate I have included common names, too. Forgetting a plant's name need not stand in your way when it comes to being able to grow it.

Above all, the *How to Garden* books are designed to fill you with passion and enthusiasm for your garden and all that its creation and care entails, from designing and planting it to maintaining it and enjoying it. For more than fifty years gardening has been my passion, and that initial enthusiasm for watching plants grow, for trying something new and for just being outside pottering has never faded. If anything I am keener on gardening now than I ever was and get more satisfaction from my plants every day. It's not that I am simply a romantic, but rather that I have learned to look for the good in gardens and in plants, and there is lots to be found. Oh, there are times when I fail – when my plants don't grow as well as they should and I need to try harder. But where would I rather be on a sunny day? Nowhere!

The *How to Garden* handbooks will, I hope, allow some of that enthusiasm – childish though it may be – to rub off on you, and the information they contain will, I hope, make you a better gardener, as well as opening your eyes to the magic of plants and flowers.

Introducing trees

Trees tend to inspire tremendous affection and respect, but as gardeners we are sometimes a bit afraid of them. Maybe it's because they live longer, and can soon become bigger than us. We may worry that they'll get out of control: picking the wrong tree, or putting it in the wrong place, can certainly have more far-reaching consequences than planting the wrong sort of rose or tulip. Selecting trees for a small garden may seem particularly fraught with difficulty. But the pages that follow will dispel those fears and give you confidence in choosing, planting and looking after trees. It's one of the best things you can do, for your garden and for the planet.

Why trees?

Almost any garden – however small – will be all the better for a tree. More than any other kind of plant, trees have the ability to change the look and feel of an outdoor space in all sorts of ways, but their benefits do not end there. As we all know, they improve the environment, the air we breathe and – not least – our state of mind. We may also hear about potential drawbacks, but plant the right tree in the right place (very important!) and you'll find the advantages will easily outweigh any problems.

Trees for towns

A town or city without any trees would be a bleak and soulless place. We may sometimes take city trees for granted, but everyone benefits from the beautifying and softening effect that trees have on the built environment, and every urban garden, right down to the smallest, can play its part in contributing to a town's 'green lung'.

If some new invention claimed to do everything that trees do to make cities better places, we'd never believe it. Trees, however small, help to absorb urban noise and pollution, magically recycling carbon dioxide into oxygen. Even small trees help keep buildings shaded and cool in summer, provide shelter from cold winds, and mop up excess rainfall, helping to reduce the problematic runoff from roads and driveways that is making flooding ever more commonplace. Trees offer a refuge to beleaguered urban wildlife, especially where a number of like-minded gardeners may, through combined planting efforts, create a significant area of wildlife habitat and a network of cover to help birds, animals and insects move safely from place to place.

Trees in the country

Trees are every bit as important in rural gardens. Modern farming methods have resulted in huge habitat loss in the countryside over the past half-century, and rural wildlife, from butterflies to frogs, is now on the decline. Country gardens with trees and hedges are becoming increasingly precious as pockets of biodiversity, offering visiting insects, birds and animals the year-round food and lodging that they may otherwise be hard pressed to find today.

Suitable trees in the garden not only provide valuable shade, shelter and screening – just as they do in an urban environment – but also give the plot a sense of belonging to its landscape, which helps to bring the countryside into the garden.

Acer palmatum 'Sango-kaku' is a tree that looks lovely all year, handsome in close-up and from a distance.

Trees: shapes and sizes

Among the defining characteristics of what makes a plant a tree, shape and size usually feature prominently, even though the plants that we all recognize as trees vary enormously in both these respects. The suitability of a tree for your particular site depends on both, so it's important to have some idea of a tree's eventual shape and size before you buy.

What is a tree?

Everyone knows what a tree is – until, that is, you try defining one and find that the more precisely you try to pin down the essential characteristics, the harder it becomes. Many (but not all) trees have a single woody stem for part of their height. Often (but not always) that stem is bare. Almost all trees are more than, say, 3m (10ft) tall when mature, but so are many shrubs, and a plant with the right characteristics is no less a tree because it doesn't reach the required height. Most of the plants included in this book are unquestionably trees, but a few that could just as easily be called shrubs are included if they have the same qualities and uses as trees – particularly in a small garden (*see* opposite, The trees in this book).

Tree shapes

Classifying trees by shape is an imprecise business. There are so many variables, and different trees of the same species will vary in both shape and size according to their position and growing conditions; for example, trees grown in a group tend to be taller and less bushy than those that are standing alone. Also, the shape of a mature tree will often be quite different from that of the 'infant' one that you buy. However, it's possible, and very useful, to have an approximate idea of the likely shape of a tree at maturity. Along with size and vigour, shape is – or should be – an important factor in determining whether the tree will suit the place you have in mind. In a small garden, a tree that is taller than it is broad will often be a

Fagus sylvatica 'Dawyck Purple' is a tall, narrow beech cultivar, popular for its distinctive dark foliage.

good choice, taking up less lateral space and casting less shade than a broad, spreading tree. But sometimes a spreading tree may provide the screening you need, and if its canopy is light and the space under it is usable, its shape needn't be a problem. *See also* page 27.

Tree shapes

Young trees may start out looking quite similar but, as they mature, most will tend towards one of these basic shapes. This will be an important factor in your choice of tree, especially for a smaller garden.

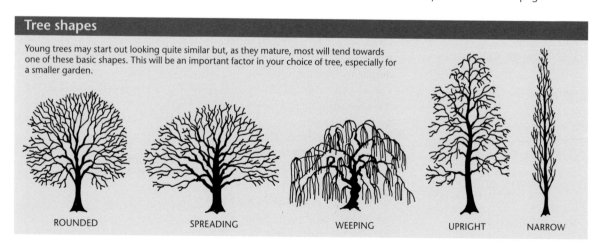

ROUNDED　　　SPREADING　　　WEEPING　　　UPRIGHT　　NARROW

ROUNDED
(width of crown roughly equal to height)

Acer campestre

Arbutus unedo

Cercis siliquastrum

Prunus lusitanica

Sorbus aria 'Lutescens'

SPREADING
(width of crown greater than height)

Catalpa bignonioides 'Aurea'

Crataegus persimilis 'Prunifolia'

Ficus carica

Koelreuteria paniculata

Parrotia persica

WEEPING
(width often greater than height;
branches may reach the ground)

Betula pendula 'Youngii'

Fagus sylvatica 'Purpurea Pendula'

Prunus 'Kiku-shidare-zakura'

Pyrus salicifolia 'Pendula'

Salix caprea 'Kilmarnock'

UPRIGHT
(height greater than width)

Azara microphylla

Betula pendula

Prunus sargentii 'Rancho'

Pyrus calleryana 'Chanticleer'

Sorbus 'Autumn Spire'

NARROW ('columnar' or 'fastigiate')
(height much greater than width)

Cupressus sempervirens

Eucryphia × nymansensis 'Nymansay'

Juniperus communis 'Hibernica'

Prunus 'Spire'

Taxus baccata 'Fastigiata'

Not-quite trees

Some plants reach tree-like proportions but do not count as trees because they are not woody. These include bamboos, tree ferns such as *Dicksonia antarctica*, and bananas like *Musa basjoo* (actually large herbaceous plants). Along with a range of readily available architectural plants, these can work well in a small space as alternatives to trees. Even when not completely hardy, they may survive winter in a mild, sheltered garden.

The various types of amelanchier tick all the boxes for small garden trees: compact, disease-resistant and with several seasons of interest.

The trees in this book

Tree sizes can be a minefield of variables, and categorizing a tree as small, medium or large purely by its height is not always very helpful. Some potentially tall trees are very slender, or grow very slowly, or can easily be kept compact and manageable by occasional pruning. Others may have a light canopy with plenty of usable space beneath. All these characteristics help to make a tree worth growing in a small space, despite its eventual height.

It is much easier to specify trees that are *not* suitable for small gardens. These would include most of the larger woodland trees, such as oaks, ashes and limes, simply because they eventually grow too big; vigorous trees with invasive roots, such as large poplars and willows; and big trees that cast dense shade, such as beeches, sycamores and all of the larger conifers. But then, in the case of the majority of these trees, certain compact, manageable cultivars have been developed that may suit a small space very well.

The easiest way to define the trees chosen for inclusion in this book is that they should be suitable for what we have defined in this series of books as a 'small garden': a plot no larger than a tennis court (roughly 260 square metres/310 square yards). In practice, this means that few of the trees in this book would eventually exceed about 10–15m (30–50ft). Many are much smaller.

Don't forget

Some weeping trees are appealing because they do not grow tall. Bear in mind, however, the loss of space underneath when the mature canopy reaches to the ground. A taller tree with usable space under it may be a better bet.

Using trees

It goes without saying that trees, as the largest and most important plants in a garden, should be pleasing to look at. They should also work hard to help make your garden the kind of space you want it to be, from a visual as well as a practical perspective. Trees are immensely valuable tools for achieving particular results: dividing spaces; making a haven for wildlife; providing shelter from the wind or a shady retreat to sit in; or screening out unwanted views while framing attractive ones.

Trees for screening

Most of us like to have at least one part of the garden that feels secluded and private. With clever planning and well-placed screening, it is perfectly possible to create a green, secret-feeling sanctuary even in a space that's hemmed in by buildings. There's nothing quite like trees to create that feeling of being cocooned in your own leafy retreat. What's more, it is now 'officially' recognized that regularly spending even a few minutes in a calming, green outdoor environment can be very therapeutic, and will have a measurably beneficial effect on our stress levels.

Deciduous or evergreen?

Many people's first thought regarding screening is that it must be evergreen: this is perhaps the reason why the appearance of fast-growing leylandii hedging was greeted with such enthusiasm some years ago. But the problems caused by × *Cuprocyparis leylandii* (to give it its proper name) are a useful reminder of why evergreen trees aren't always the answer. As they mature, they tend to blot out what you do want to see – sky and sunshine – as well as what you don't. Worse, large evergreens keep out precious sunlight in winter, when the sun is low in the sky, even more than they do in summer. And the deep, year-round shade cast by tall evergreens is not a hospitable environment for other plants.

There will be some circumstances where it's essential to have screening

Choosing trees for screening

Most trees can be employed as an effective screen, but some will provide cover for a longer season than others. *Crataegus × lavalleei* 'Carrierei' usually hangs on to its leaves for some time after most other trees are bare, giving cover well into winter. Early-flowering *Prunus* species, such as the cherry plum (*Prunus cerasifera*), are already producing some screening effect by late winter with their early blossom, which is soon followed by the opening leaves. Birch makes a hazy screen even when leafless, especially when its mass of fine twigs is spangled with raindrops. The effect is boosted when the small but numerous catkins begin to swell in late winter.

These Himalayan birches show how screening can be light and airy, and very stylish – but still highly effective.

throughout the year, particularly where something you would rather not have to look at is spoiling the view from your house. This might be an ugly building, a prominent structure such as a phone mast, or your neighbour's old van. The impact of such eyesores tends to be greater in winter, when views are not softened by greenery, and for effective screening you will probably need some kind of evergreen. However, for the most part, deciduous trees are more practical and make a more attractive screen that will provide a sense of seclusion through the months when you spend time in the garden, but will let in welcome light in winter, when the branches are bare.

Another point worth remembering when planning screening is that it may not be essential, in every case, to blot out an unwanted view completely. Interrupting a view by placing a focal point, such as a striking small tree or shrub, in the foreground to distract the eye from something further away can be surprisingly effective. And although positioning a tree with a light canopy in front may not obscure the eyesore completely, it will certainly break up its outline sufficiently to draw attention to the tree, rather than to what's behind it.

The eye-catching mop-headed tree here is *Catalpa bignonioides*, pruned regularly to make a compact specimen: perfect for a smaller space.

Don't forget

A tree that is positioned close to a viewpoint, such as a window or outdoor seating area, will obscure a larger percentage of your field of vision than one positioned immediately in front of an object you want to hide. For the most effective screening of large objects, plant a tree or trees in the foreground.

Pleached trees

A row of pleached trees makes a very pleasing eye-level screen without losing too much garden space. Like a hedge on stilts, it will provide dense, leafy cover in summer and a more subtle but still attractive filigree screen of bare twigs after leaf fall. Pleaching entails pruning the trees to leave clear stems up to a height of about 1.2–1.5m (4–5ft). Branches above that level are trained on a framework of horizontal wires, growing to meet the branches of neighbouring trees and maybe eventually fusing with them. Often, the resulting eye-level 'hedge' is clipped into a formal shape, making the practice especially suitable for more formal gardens – though it can take some years for the feature to reach maturity. Hornbeam (*Carpinus betulus*, shown right) and lime (*Tilia × euchlora* is best) are the trees most often used for pleaching, but many others are suitable. Fruit trees, such as pears, can be trained into eye-level espaliers, and holly, yew or box will make an evergreen screen.

If you enjoy eating fruit (and maybe if you don't), there's a lot to be said for growing at least one fruit tree – even if it's your only tree. Fruit trees tend to be attractively shaped and compact, and most of them offer at least two seasons of beauty, in the form of spring blossom and autumn fruit. A tree such as an apple or a pear gives a garden a sense of permanence and purpose. Your garden wildlife will thank you for it, too.

Keeping fruit trees compact

Fruit trees have a further advantage over many other trees for small gardens: their compact size – usually because they have been grown not on their own roots but on dwarfing rootstocks. A venerable old apple, pear or plum can be a beautiful tree, but fruit trees grown on their own roots tend to become too large for most gardens, and they also crop reliably only as mature trees, which can mean a very long wait before you pick your first apple. For many years, growers have raised fruit trees suitable for both gardens and commercial orchards by grafting particular varieties onto special rootstocks that enable young trees to produce a crop (*see* box, right). The choice of rootstock also makes the vigour and final size of the fruit tree more predictable.

Rootstocks

Apples are most often sold on the semi-dwarfing rootstock M26, which is likely to produce a freestanding tree with a mature height of some 2–3m (6–10ft). M26 has enough vigour for cordons and for fruit trees in pots. The semi-dwarfing MM106 produces larger trees. M116 is valuable for its drought tolerance and carries some disease resistance. Where a really dwarfing rootstock is needed – for a miniature tree on fertile soil, for example – look for M27; firm staking will be needed throughout the tree's life to keep roots stable. M27 is not robust enough to provide the necessary nourishment for fruit in pots.

The usual rootstocks for pears are: Quince A, good on poor soil or for weaker-growing varieties; and Quince C, good on fertile soil. Plums, gages, peaches and apricots are most often grafted onto St Julien A (an all-rounder) or Pixy (smaller, but needing good soil). Cherries are usually grafted on to a rootstock of medium vigour named Colt.

Trained fruit trees

Many ingenious training methods have been developed for creating neat, productive fruit trees in restricted spaces. These are the tried and tested classic shapes most often used; they are ornamental as well as practical. Once the tree's basic framework is established, pruning mainly involves shortening the sideshoots in summer to encourage 'fruiting spurs' and promote ripening.

STEPOVER

CORDON

FAN

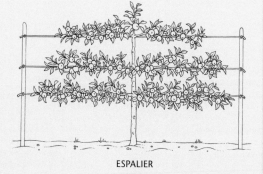

ESPALIER

CORDON A single main stem is trained either vertically or at an angle of 45 degrees. Fruiting spurs (short stubs on which fruit buds appear) are encouraged to form along its length.

FAN The tree is grown flat against a supporting fence or wall, with the branches trained to fan out from the top of a short trunk. The fruiting spurs form on the branches.

ESPALIER This is like a fan in that the branch structure is grown flat, but several tiers of branches are trained symmetrically along horizontal wires to either side of a single main stem.

STEPOVER One tier of branches is trained horizontally at just 30cm (12in) or so above the ground. Stepovers can be used to make an attractive edging for vegetable or salad beds.

Trees for fruit

There has long been a whole branch of horticulture devoted to obtaining a bumper fruit crop from a small space, so if it is the fruit itself that is the main attraction, you will easily find a tree to provide it, however tiny your plot. Alongside dwarfing rootstocks, numerous pruning techniques have been developed over the years to maximize crops while keeping trees compact and attractive. Fruit trees that are trained against walls or on a freestanding framework as cordons, fans, espaliers or stepovers (*see* opposite) take up very little space and can be highly productive. Training on a south-facing wall is especially valuable for sun-loving fruits such as apricots, peaches and figs, which ripen more reliably if given warmth and shelter.

Pollination

Many stone fruits, including plums and cherries, are at least partially self-fertile (that is, the flowers can pollinate themselves or other flowers on the same plant), so having only one tree need not be a problem. Apples and pears, on the other hand, need a pollinating partner. The whole business of pollination is something of a minefield. Issues of compatibility and timing are much discussed in gardening books, and ideally you would plant at least two compatible trees that flower simultaneously, such as the apples 'Sunset' and 'Fiesta', or

the pears 'Beth' and 'Concorde'. But with luck, help will be at hand from fruit trees in neighbouring gardens. A fairly recent solution is the 'family tree', where several different apple or pear varieties have been grafted one above the other onto a single tree. Buy family trees from a reputable supplier to ensure you get compatible varieties of comparable vigour.

Fruit trees in containers

Given adequate water and food, most kinds of fruit tree can be grown in large pots. The container itself will, however, restrict the tree's size to some extent, so it's not necessary to choose trees grown on a very dwarfing rootstock.

Your own sun-ripened fruit straight from the tree is a really special treat.

① 'Oullins Gage' is an old favourite dessert plum of outstanding flavour.

② 'James Grieve' and 'Elstar' apples here grow together on a family tree.

③ This juicy apple variety 'Fiesta' is growing happily in a large pot.

Use loam-based compost, which has a bit of weight to it, and stake the tree securely. If you can, choose a spot out of the wind but with plenty of sunshine, and turn the pot from time to time to ensure light reaches all sides. Maintenance is simple: top-dress the surface with fresh compost each spring, feed annually with slow-release, high-potash fertilizer, and never let your tree go short of water.

> **Don't forget**
>
> In summer, carefully thin each cluster of fruit such as apples and pears to one or two fruits, to improve fruit quality. Removing a few leaves around the fruit will also enhance the colour and promote ripening.

If you plan your layout around existing mature trees, you can ensure they will become a major asset to the garden.

least for part of the day, all year round. The position and nature of that kind of shade are difficult to control or change, but shade cast by trees is a different matter. First, the trees themselves make a positive contribution to the beauty of the garden; second, you can position them where you wish. You can also choose what kind of shade you would like to have – light, dappled or dense. And the area of shade can be determined by how large a tree you plant, and whether (and how) you prune it to control its size.

Trees to sit under

Whether it's for a whole afternoon or just a snatched moment, relaxing in the dappled shade under a tree on a hot day is one of those special treats that are worth planning for.

Trees to provide shade

Shade is usually seen as a problem in the garden, and too much can be very difficult to deal with. But gardens with too little shade are problematic in other ways. Lacking variety and a sense of depth, they can also look uninteresting – especially in the flat glare of the summer sun. Many plants struggle without any shade, and worst of all there is nowhere comfortable and refreshing to sit, or to potter among the plants, on a hot summer's day.

Most gardens have some shade from buildings and from their own boundary fences, walls or hedges, at

Using your trees for garden projects

Gardens aren't the place for any major kind of forestry enterprise, but don't let that put you off taking advantage of simple home-grown materials that you can use for plant supports and other garden structures such as wigwams, woven fencing or perhaps a rustic arch.

Hazel is the prime candidate for the job. Each plant will need a growing space of

about 2 x 2m (6 x 6ft). You may have to wait several years for your first crop but, after that, three or four hazel plants, each coppiced (cut to the ground) in rotation every fifth winter or so, should supply you with a few tall, straight poles and plenty of pea sticks each year. It's a great way to garden sustainably, and natural plant supports – such as bean-poles and twiggy sticks of various lengths to support climbers (including sweet peas) and herbaceous plants – look more attractive and can work better than their artificial (and often expensive) factory-made counterparts.

If you keep its vigorous growth habit under control, willow (shown left) is also good for certain uses, including woven panels or edging for beds and paths, and for arbours, obelisks and sculptures. When regularly coppiced, varieties with coloured stems will also provide winter interest.

A frame of mature trees makes all the difference to a seat or arbour, giving it not only summer shade but also a visual anchor and a sense of belonging.

Placing a seat under a suitable tree immediately creates a kind of outdoor room, its mood dominated by the unique quality of the gently moving leaves overhead. Tree and seat become a focal point to be looked at, as well as a viewpoint to look out from.

From both aspects, a spreading tree is the best option, with a leaf canopy that transmits a fair amount of light: an apple tree is a classic choice or, if you want to try something a bit more unusual, consider a multi-stemmed *Catalpa bignonioides* 'Aurea'. This has a

Don't forget

It is hard to be objective about a space you look at every day, and a fresh eye can be of tremendous value when weighing up your garden with a view to planting for shade or screening. Take photos – they often highlight problem features you may not have noticed.

pleasing, spreading shape and gives an uplifting quality of light through its large, golden leaves.

Trees as windbreaks

Usually thought of in connection with large gardens in open countryside, perhaps near the sea, windbreaks call to mind rows of tough trees and shrubs planted to reduce the wind's force, but wind can be a problem in town gardens, too. Buildings, and the gaps between them, can create downdraughts and eddies that can wreak havoc in what might otherwise be a sheltered garden. The panelled or close-boarded fences so often used along boundaries can make the problem

worse because the solid nature of such structures just makes the wind bounce off, creating turbulence where you least expect it. Trees and shrubs are much more effective at filtering and slowing down the wind, shielding both you and your plants as well as providing comfortable shelter. When you are planning your garden, take time to observe how it is affected by winds from different directions and notice the turbulence they cause. Sometimes, for example, wind from a particular direction will tend to blow plants away from a wall or even knock potted plants over. A tree or two, strategically positioned so as to interrupt the path of the incoming wind, may well solve the problem.

A suitable tree is probably the single best thing you could plant to bring wildlife into your garden. Birds will love to perch in it and, as it grows larger, may nest in it or feed on its store of tasty morsels, from caterpillars and aphids to autumn berries and seeds. Help draw them in by hanging feeders in the tree or by installing a nest box. Generally speaking, native trees are the most wildlife-friendly. Oak, ash and many others are, of course, much too big for most gardens, but that still leaves a surprisingly wide choice on offer, even if your plot is very small.

Provide bees with apple blossom and they'll work hard to give you a crop.

Trees and wildlife habitats

One of the richest wild habitats is what ecologists call 'woodland edge'. As the name suggests, this is the rich and varied area on the margins of a wood: it includes trees and shrubs for shelter and shade, next to open areas and sunny glades, where both flowering plants and insects such as butterflies and bees can flourish. A group of gardens is like a woodland edge, and as wild habitats become more threatened and degraded, so gardens – urban and rural – are gaining in importance as a refuge for wildlife.

One vital role that trees play is to link gardens together, to connect breeding populations of birds and insects. Most individual gardens don't have the space or the variety to support viable populations of wild creatures, but several gardens together can make a real difference, and trees are a key component of the resulting ecosystem.

Choosing a tree

The first step is to choose a species of tree that will suit your conditions and space. If there is room, a birch or a rowan is a good choice for light soil, or perhaps an alder for a damp garden. Hawthorn is a great survivor on difficult sites of all types, and will enliven the garden with clouds of fragrant blossom and heavy crops of autumn berries that will attract blackbirds and thrushes as winter sets in. Bees are irresistibly drawn to trees with early blossom in spring: a cherry or a pear, maybe, or a goat willow (*Salix caprea*) if space permits.

Hazel (*Corylus avellana*) is a winner in small spaces, as it can be coppiced

Nest boxes

Many different designs of nest box are on sale, or you can make your own. The design and the size of the hole will determine the species that might be tempted to use it: a small, round hole no more than 25mm (1in) across for blue tits; slightly larger for great tits and house sparrows, and an open-fronted box for robins and wrens. Secure the box to the tree trunk at least 2m (6ft) from the ground, in the hope of deterring cats. The hole should face east or north, away from hot sun and wet winds. Install the box in winter, to give birds time to explore and get used to it. After the breeding season, clear out old nest debris in time for the new occupants.

A good nest box in the right place will usually find a customer.

(*see* pages 51–2) to control its size and to let light into the space underneath it, allowing woodland flowers such as primroses, violets and bluebells to bloom in spring and supply nectar for early bees.

Other small trees and shrubs to consider include spindle (*Euonymus europaeus*), a tree-like shrub that dazzles in autumn with its fluorescent pink-and-orange fruits and scarlet leaves. It grows well on chalky soil, as does buckthorn (*Rhamnus cathartica*), a small, spiny, berrying tree or shrub that is the food plant of the brimstone butterfly. The related alder buckthorn (*Frangula alnus*) also feeds the green caterpillars of these delicate yellow butterflies, which overwinter as adults and are usually the first to be enticed out by early spring sunshine. More suited to damper, acid soils, alder buckthorn makes a pleasing small tree, with dark bark and red berries that change to black – striking when both colours are on the tree together.

Native evergreens

Familiar garden plants include several native evergreen trees, for example yew, holly and box. These offer all-important winter cover for birds and insects, as well as permanent structure in the garden. Yew and holly, if they are left unclipped, produce glowing red berries much enjoyed by blackbirds and thrushes, as well as by fieldfares and redwings – more

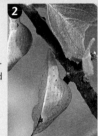

Trees are a natural larder for many garden creatures.

① Holly berries are a favourite of blackbirds.

② Brimstones feed and pupate on buckthorn.

③ The fleshy seed coat of spindle berries is enjoyed by robins.

Tree stumps and log piles

A tree's usefulness to wildlife does not end when it dies. Dead wood offers food and shelter to a host of invertebrates from beetle larvae to wasps, woodlice and centipedes. A tucked-away corner with a log pile or tree stump may attract woodpeckers, frogs and hedgehogs in search of a meal. Mosses and ferns may make their home in it too.

unusual winter visitors to gardens. Holly may well attract the delightful holly blue butterfly, which favours garden hollies in spring as food for its first brood but, curiously, chooses ivy for its second.

Yew, holly and box are all shade-tolerant. They are also very forgiving when clipped repeatedly, so they are useful for topiary and can be shaped into compact, tree-like plants to suit even the tiniest space.

More trees for wildlife

Acer campestre
Amelanchier lamarckii
Betula pendula
Genista aetnensis
Malus domestica
Morus nigra
Sorbus aucuparia

Don't forget

Obsessive tidiness and wildlife tend not to go together. Don't be too keen to sweep up every fallen leaf in autumn: leaf litter blown into odd corners provides winter cover for hedgehogs, amphibians, reptiles and many beneficial insects from ground beetles to ladybirds.

Trees for all seasons

There is no reason why trees can't be making some contribution to the beauty of a garden on every day of the year, from the earliest catkins to the last of the autumn leaves; and when these fall, the handsome bark can be revealed. The challenge with a small space, of course, is to fit it all in. But a carefully chosen single tree can earn its keep over many months, and if you have room for two or three more, you can easily have something enticing to look at on a daily basis.

Salix caprea 'Kilmarnock' is a star in late winter, but hard to love later in the year, when it can look drab.

Malus floribunda is hard *not* to love, with its dainty apple blossoms and healthy constitution.

Early flowers and catkins

Long before the arrival of spring, keen gardeners are eagerly watching out for signs of activity as plants respond to the lengthening days. Finding room for a couple of trees that offer late-winter cheer will give rewards out of all proportion to the space they occupy. Catkins on hazels and alders are in place by leaf fall, but it's encouraging to watch them expand in the early days of the year, and to be the first to spot the minute red flowers on hazel twigs, which eventually become nuts. Pussy willow is a favourite in the early-spring countryside, and its garden counterpart, *Salix caprea* 'Kilmarnock', is small enough to be grown in a pot.

Witch hazel (*Hamamelis*) is one of the earliest woody plants to flower, with its curious spidery, fragrant blooms in shades of yellow or orange according to cultivar. With

very little pruning, it will over time form an attractive, open shuttlecock shape, with golden autumn foliage for a second season of interest. Try to position the tree where both flowers and autumn leaves will be set aglow by low, late-afternoon sunshine. Other early flowers are to be found on Cornelian cherry (*Cornus mas*), *Prunus incisa* and *Prunus × subhirtella* 'Autumnalis'.

Spring blossom

There is nothing quite like the magic of a bare-branched tree suddenly coming to glorious life after many cold, dreary months of passing almost unnoticed as a drab skeleton.

Colour combinations

With the great variety of spring blossom, there is much scope for unintended colour clashes when two plants flower simultaneously but don't do one another any favours. For example, the strong yellow of laburnum looks better alone or with quieter neighbours, rather than mixing with strident pinks and lilacs. Forsythia and flowering cherries sometimes make an ill-matched pair.

When clouds of pink and white blossom are transforming gardens, parks and streets everywhere, it's certainly a moment to savour, but in a small garden it makes sense to choose trees that have more than one such moment of glory in the year. Luckily, a good many flowering cherries and crab apples, for example, also have attractive fruits and/or foliage in the autumn (*see* pages 22–3). Remember too that if you have space for two or more trees you can enjoy blossom for several months in succession, provided you plan carefully. For instance, hawthorn or lilac might take over from the cherries and plums as their blossom begins to fade, or an apple tree from an amelanchier or magnolia.

Spring foliage

Though it is showy blossom that tends to get all the attention in spring, the subtler beauty of unadulterated, brand-new green is just as uplifting. Birches, hawthorns

Fagus sylvatica 'Dawyck Purple' has all the glory of copper beech foliage on a more compact, upright tree.

The red buckeye (here, *Aesculus pavia* 'Humilis') is small in stature, but big on spring drama.

Crinodendrum hookerianum is one to try for summer flowers if you can give it the right soil – acid and moist.

and maples look particularly fresh as their leaves open. Beeches, a little later to burst, have silky, translucent young leaves of either soft green or (in the case of purple cultivars) coppery pink. The average garden is no place for most forms of the common beech (*Fagus sylvatica*) – at up to 40m (130ft), it is one of Britain's tallest native trees – but its fastigiate forms (upright with closely set, upswept branches) are more manageable. 'Dawyck', 'Dawyck Purple' and 'Dawyck Gold' all start off very slim and upright, growing quite slowly into tall but broader columnar trees. Another possibility would be one of the compact forms of weeping beech, such as the purple-leaved *Fagus sylvatica* 'Purpurea Pendula'. Although it is a small tree, its distinctive dome shape

and dark colour draw the eye. It needs the right setting to look its best and, in summer, makes a good foil for plants with 'hot' colours.

Horse chestnuts are among the most exciting spring trees. The large leaves are early to break out of their characteristic sticky buds, quickly expanding into the handsome, bright green, many-fingered leaves that are typical of the genus. A little later come the unmistakable 'candles' that make the trees look so spectacular in flower. Unfortunately, common horse chestnuts (*Aesculus hippocastanum*) are much too large for most gardens and are martyrs to several pests and diseases, but some of their American relatives are more manageable and seem to have better resistance. The red buckeye (*Aesculus pavia*) makes a tree only about 5m (16ft) tall, and its slow-growing cultivar *Aesculus pavia* var. *discolor* 'Koehnei' is only half that size. Perhaps the most striking ornamental horse chestnut in spring is *Aesculus × neglecta* 'Erythroblastos',

a hybrid whose young foliage is a dazzling apricot colour. It prefers a sheltered, partially shaded spot.

Summer flowers

Although spring is the season most associated with blossom, there is something rather special about a tree that is full of flowers in high summer. Some of these are tricky to grow, but if you have garden conditions to suit their exacting demands they are really a sight to behold. They are best positioned where they can hog the limelight at a time when other plants will be vying for attention.

Mild, sheltered gardens with moist acid soil (such as those found in the south west of Britain and the west coast of Ireland) are good places to try *Crinodendron hookerianum.* This rather shrub-like small tree from Chile becomes quite a conversation piece for several weeks over summer when festooned with deep-red lanterns, set off to perfection by the dark evergreen foliage. You could

The little-known hawthorn *Crataegus orientalis* is an ideal tree for a small, sunny garden.

Most crab apple trees are quite compact, with flowers and fruit to give different seasons of interest.

try growing it in a container (using ericaceous compost) in a sheltered, semi-shaded spot: it flowers from quite a young age.

A tree that shows a charmingly defiant spirit by clinging on to summer when others have moved towards producing autumn fruits and foliage tints is the golden rain tree (*Koelreuteria paniculata*). Its golden-yellow flowers could have been tailor-made to shine in low late-summer sunlight, and its large, interestingly shaped leaves make it

a pleasure to look at all through the growing season. The flowers are replaced by intriguing, inflated, pinkish seedpods. Other summer-flowering trees include *Albizia julibrissin*, *Styrax japonicus* and the various kinds of *Eucryphia*, whose flowers are irresistible to bees.

Berries and fruits

Berries are a mainstay of the autumn garden, providing a blaze of colour on sunny days and a burst of good cheer on dull ones. Rowans, hollies

and hawthorns are the principal providers in the world of small garden trees, but don't forget the ornamental value of crab apples too (*see* pages 82–3). All are winter staples for birds, drawing in blackbirds and thrushes on cold days and keeping the garden full of life, at least until the trees are bare. Don't overlook the berries that are more unusual and visually interesting (*see* box, opposite, and page 27).

Autumn leaf colour

Most maples are masters of autumn colour, setting gardens ablaze everywhere and starring in the legendary 'leaf-peeping' tours of the north-eastern USA. The celebrated American natives such as the sugar maple (*Acer saccharum*) grow far too large for most gardens, but some of the Japanese maples (cultivars of *Acer palmatum*) make perfect courtyard-sized substitutes. Few reach more than 5m (16ft) tall – many are smaller – and some cultivars take the form of dumpy shrubs rather than trees. Their elegant, hand-shaped leaves make them worthy of a semi-shaded, sheltered spot at any time but especially in autumn. 'Osakazuki' is a tried-and-tested cultivar for autumn colour, with a rather spreading shape and seven-lobed leaves that turn fiery red, as do those of the more upright 'Shishigashira'. For soft-yellow leaves on an upright plant, the old faithful 'Sango-kaku' is hard to beat for a restricted space, while for larger gardens there is the native field maple, *Acer campestre*, which ends the season in a brief blaze of pure gold.

A touch of the exotic

The exotic style of gardening has in recent years become rather popular. It uses bold, luxuriant foliage and sultry, tropical colours in jungle-like schemes that are at their peak in late summer and autumn. Some of the trees or tree-like shrubs (not all of which are completely hardy) that can help provide the backbone for such schemes are:

Abutilon megapotamicum
Ailanthus altissima (coppiced)
Callistemon salignus; *Callistemon viminalis*
Catalpa bignonioides 'Aurea' (coppiced)

Citrus limon
Cordyline australis
Cotinus coggygria
Eriobotrya japonica
Eucalyptus gunnii (coppiced)
Ficus carica
Paulownia tomentosa (coppiced)
Pseudopanax ferox
Rhus typhina
Trachycarpus fortunei
Yucca gloriosa

Just as with spring blossom, colourful autumn foliage, however splendid it may be, is often short-lived, and if the tree looks pretty ordinary for the rest of the year you can't really justify giving it space in a small garden. Fortunately, many small trees have autumn colour as a second string to their bow. Amelanchiers, for instance, are handsome in both spring and autumn, and their compact shape and dainty flowers, little berries and foliage make them an all-year asset. Certain varieties of *Prunus* colour well in autumn, as does the flowering crab apple *Malus tschonoskii*. There are rowan and hawthorn cultivars, too (for example *Sorbus* 'Chinese Lace' or *Sorbus commixta* 'Olympic Flame', *Crataegus crus-galli* and *Crataegus persimilis* 'Prunifolia') that tick all three boxes: spring blossom, abundant berries and colourful leaves in autumn.

See also Design palette, page 27.

One of the Japanese maples – elegant all spring and summer, building slowly to an autumn spectacle.

Unusual berries

If you are looking for some out-of-the-ordinary autumn drama, consider *Clerodendrum trichotomum* var. *fargesii*, which has extraordinary blue berries (shown above); spindle (*Euonymus europaeus*, see page 67), with showy pink fruit; or *Callicarpa bodinieri* var. *giraldii* 'Profusion' (see page 53), for its masses of violet-purple berries. These plants are all more usually thought of as shrubs but, with appropriate pruning, will form unusual small trees (see page 53).

Winter bark

Tree bark often passes unnoticed, but as more and more people look to their gardens to provide interest all year round, trees that offer this winter bonus are becoming popular and more widely appreciated. The Himalayan birch (*Betula utilis* var. *jacquemontii*), wth its shining white bark, has become a bit of a classic, lending itself to many styles of garden including contemporary schemes. It is equally effective as a single-stemmed or multi-stemmed tree, or – where there is room – in a group. But you may be surprised at just how big the Himalayan birch can ultimately grow, and for most gardens it is worth seeking out one of the more compact cultivars, such as *Betula utilis* var. *jacquemontii* 'Grayswood Ghost'. Tree nurseries have selected several other fine birches that have decorative bark; stars include the copper-pink, satiny bark of *Betula albosinensis* 'Fascination' and the exceptionally

Acer capillipes is one of several species known as snake-bark maples – all excellent for winter interest.

flaky and peeling, pinkish-buff bark of *Betula nigra* 'Heritage'. Their warm tones are really set aglow by low winter sunshine. Other trees with reddish or bronze bark include *Prunus maackii* 'Amber Beauty', *Prunus serrula* and *Acer griseum*.

Another group of trees that reveal handsome bark after leaf fall are the snake-bark maples. Their trunks and branches have subtle vertical striations in shades of green and silver or white. They include *Acer davidii* and *Acer capillipes*. Moosewood (*Acer pensylvanicum*) is another – although it can be tricky to grow and prefers acid soil. Try to get the tree established when young and protect it from hot sun and chilly winds.

See page 27 for more suggestions.

Don't forget

Plant a tree with interesting winter bark where you will have the chance to appreciate its texture and colour in close-up, either from a window or as you walk past it in the garden.

Colour and light

When deciding where to plant a tree, try to position it for maximum colour impact. For example, several stems of the white-barked Himalayan birch *Betula utilis* var. *jacquemontii* 'Grayswood Ghost', or the silvered spring foliage of *Sorbus aria* 'Lutescens', will look luminous against a dark background such as a shady wall or yew hedge. A tree with warm reddish bark, such as a yew or a paper-bark maple (*Acer griseum*), becomes a really striking feature if you place it where it will be bathed in low, late-afternoon sunshine on a winter's day. The same applies to *Alnus incana* 'Aurea', an alder with dashing orange-red catkins. The fresh green foliage of early summer looks its best where it is caught by morning sunshine; white blossom looks magical from a doorway or window at dusk; and the impact of golden foliage is greatest where it is flooded by the rich, early-evening light of late summer.

Sited against a dark background, *Sorbus aria* 'Lutescens' makes a memorable feature as its silvery leaves catch and reflect the light.

Ten all-rounders

Many trees perform in more than one season, but those listed here are the really hard-working ones that earn their keep by providing interesting flowers, fruit, berries, foliage or bark at different times of year.

TREE	SPRING	SUMMER	AUTUMN	WINTER
Acer griseum	Foliage	Foliage	Foliage	Bark
Acer palmatum 'Sango-kaku'	Foliage	Foliage	Foliage	Bark
Amelanchier lamarckii	Blossom	Berries	Foliage	
Betula pendula	Catkins	Foliage	Foliage	Bark
Cercis siliquastrum	Blossom	Foliage	Foliage	
Cornus controversa 'Variegata'	Blossom	Foliage	Foliage	
Crataegus orientalis	Blossom	Foliage	Berries	Berries
Malus domestica 'Fiesta' (dessert apple)	Blossom		Fruit	
Sorbus aucuparia 'Sheerwater Seedling'	Blossom	Foliage	Berries	
Taxus baccata 'Fastigiata'	Foliage	Berries	Berries	Foliage

Evergreen trees

In a small garden, think hard before planting an evergreen tree: most cast deep shade that can change the garden's character and make it difficult for other plants to flourish. Sometimes, however, an evergreen tree will be just the answer, provided you select wisely and make sure you keep its growth in check.

Some evergreens have very useful characteristics:
① The leaves of *Prunus lusitanica* are shiny green.
② *Ilex aquifolium* 'J.C. van Tol' is good for berries.
③ *Cupressus sempervirens* is a slim eye-catcher.

Evergreen trees for screening

If you have decided that an evergreen is the only way to hide an ugly view (*see* pages 12–13), choose a tree that is handsome in its own right. The variegated Chinese privet (*Ligustrum lucidum* 'Excelsum Superbum'), with its cream-variegated leaves for a light effect and fragrant flowers in autumn, is a good bet for a small, sheltered garden. Certain other broad-leaved evergreens, such as holly (*Ilex*) and Portugal laurel (*Prunus lusitanica*), have glossy leaves that reflect light and prevent drabness. Both can be readily pruned to keep them compact. The strawberry tree (*Arbutus unedo*) also offers visual interest, with reddish bark and winter flowers and red fruits when mature. In a mild garden, an olive would be a good option: young plants are fairly fast-growing, and olive trees suggest a sunny Mediterranean hillside rather than the northern forests conjured up by many conifers.

Evergreens for structure

Box, holly and yew are three native evergreens that are invaluable in gardens. They make neat, small trees that can be clipped to any shape or size, or even hard pruned when mature. A compact topiary tree or a cloud-pruned specimen fits into the tiniest of spaces. Hollies are the most varied of the three in leaf form, ranging from the plain green, almost prickle-

free, self-fertile *Ilex aquifolium* 'J.C. van Tol' through variegated cultivars such as *Ilex × altaclerensis* 'Golden King' or *Ilex aquifolium* 'Argentea Marginata', with cream leaf margins.

Compact conifers may bring to mind rather dull 1970s heather beds, but in ones and twos they can provide very useful structure in small spaces. There is a confusing number, of every shape and size, but manageably narrow ones include: *Chamaecyparis lawsoniana* 'Columnaris', with upright sprays of blue-grey leaves; *Cupressus sempervirens* (*see* page 76); *Picea pungens* 'Koster', a conical spruce with blue-grey foliage; and *Chamaecyparis pisifera* 'Boulevard', whose soft grey-blue foliage develops purplish hues in winter. Other conifers that change colour for winter include *Thuja occidentalis* 'Rheingold', which takes on hues of antique gold, and the small tree or shrub *Cryptomeria japonica* Elegans Group, whose feathery, green foliage turns to rich bronze-purple.

For more evergreens, *see* page 38.

Cloud pruning

This idea derives from the traditional Japanese pruning craft known as *niwaki*. An evergreen is clipped into a sculptural shape with neatly trimmed nuggets ('clouds') of dense foliage supported by a strongly structural framework of bare branches. The effect is tree-like but open and 'contrasty', and a cloud-pruned specimen makes a very striking focal point that is ideal for a confined space. Many evergreens are suitable for this treatment: small-leaved trees like box, yew, certain cypresses (shown above), *Phillyrea latifolia*, *Ligustrum delavayanum* and *Luma apiculata* are among the best.

Design palette

These pages will help you choose trees for particular visual effects in the garden, giving just a few of the range of possibilities for each category. *See also* Trees for a purpose, pages 38–9, and the A–Z directory, pages 69–91.

Foliage colour

VARIEGATED

Acer negundo 'Flamingo' (right)
Acer platanoides 'Drummondii'
Cornus alternifolia 'Argentea'
Cornus controversa 'Variegata'
Cornus mas 'Variegata'
Ilex aquifolium 'Silver Queen'
Ligustrum lucidum 'Excelsum Superbum'
Salix integra 'Hakuro-nishiki'

GREY AND SILVER

Buddleja alternifolia 'Argentea'
Elaeagnus angustifolia
Eucalyptus gunnii
Hippophae rhamnoides
Olea europaea
Picea pungens 'Koster'
Pyrus salicifolia 'Pendula'
Salix exigua (right)
Sorbus aria 'Lutescens'

GOLDEN

Acer palmatum 'Sango-kaku'
Acer shirasawanum 'Aureum' (right)
Alnus incana 'Aurea'
Catalpa bignonioides 'Aurea'
Fagus sylvatica 'Dawyck Gold'
Gleditsia triacanthos 'Sunburst'
Ilex × altaclerensis 'Golden King'
Juniperus chinensis 'Aurea'
Taxus baccata Aurea Group
Ulmus × hollandica 'Dampieri Aurea'

PURPLE AND BRONZE

Acer palmatum 'Bloodgood' (right)
Catalpa × erubescens 'Purpurea'
Cercis canadensis 'Forest Pansy'
Corylus maxima 'Purpurea'
Cotinus coggygria 'Royal Purple'
Fagus sylvatica 'Dawyck Purple'
Gleditsia triacanthos 'Rubylace'
Malus 'Directeur Moerlands'
Pittosporum tenuifolium 'Purpureum'
Prunus cerasifera 'Spring Glow'

Flower colour

WHITE

Amelanchier lamarckii
Arbutus unedo
Cornus 'Eddie's White Wonder'
Crataegus monogyna
Davidia involucrata
Eucryphia × nymansensis 'Nymansay'
Halesia monticola var. vestita
Ligustrum lucidum 'Excelsum Superbum'
Luma apiculata
Magnolia × loebneri 'Merrill'
Magnolia stellata
Malus hupehensis
Malus 'John Downie'
Osmanthus × burkwoodii
Prunus 'Shirotae' (right)
Pyrus calleryana 'Chanticleer'
Sorbus aucuparia
Styrax japonicus

PINK

Aesculus pavia
Albizia julibrissin f. rosea
Cercis siliquastrum
Crataegus laevigata 'Crimson Cloud'
Magnolia 'Heaven Scent'
Malus floribunda
Malus 'Van Eseltine' (right)
Prunus cerasifera 'Spring Glow'
Prunus 'Kursar'
Robinia × slavinii 'Hillieri'

CREAM AND YELLOW

Acacia baileyana 'Purpurea'
Azara microphylla
Cornus mas
Genista aetnensis
Hamamelis mollis
Koelreuteria paniculata
Laburnum × watereri 'Vossii' (right)
Magnolia 'Elizabeth'
Prunus 'Ukon'
Sophora 'Sun King'

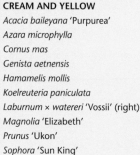

Other ornamental features

BERRIES AND FRUIT

Amelanchier lamarckii (black)

Arbutus unedo (orange and red)

Callicarpa bodinieri (purple)

Clerodendrum trichotomum var. *fargesii* (blue)

Cornus mas (red)

Cotoneaster frigidus 'Cornubia' (red)

Luma apiculata (black)

Malus × robusta 'Red Sentinel' (red)

Malus transitoria (yellow)

Sorbus cashmiriana (white)

Sorbus commixta 'Olympic Flame' (red)

Sorbus hupehensis 'Pink Pagoda' (pink)

Sorbus 'Joseph Rock' (yellow; right)

Sorbus vilmorinii (pink)

AUTUMN FOLIAGE COLOUR

Acer griseum

Acer palmatum

Amelanchier lamarckii

Malus trilobata

Mespilus germanica

Parrotia persica

Prunus 'Accolade'

Rhus typhina (right)

Sorbus 'Chinese Lace'

Sorbus commixta 'Olympic Flame'

CATKINS

Alnus glutinosa 'Imperialis'

Alnus incana 'Aurea'

Betula albosinensis 'Fascination'

Betula pendula

Corylus avellana 'Contorta' (right)

Salix caprea 'Kilmarnock'

Salix daphnoides

BARK

Acer davidii

Acer griseum (right)

Acer palmatum 'Sango-kaku'

Acer pensylvanicum

Arbutus unedo

Betula albosinensis 'Fascination'

Betula nigra 'Heritage'

Betula utilis var. *jacquemontii* 'Grayswood Ghost'

Frangula alnus

Luma apiculata

Parrotia persica

Prunus maackii 'Amber Beauty'

Prunus serrula

Form and habit

UPRIGHT

Cupressus sempervirens

Eucryphia × nymansensis 'Nymansay'

Fagus sylvatica 'Dawyck'

Ilex aquifolium 'Green Pillar'

Juniperus communis 'Hibernica'

Juniperus scopulorum 'Skyrocket'

Malus trilobata

Pinus sylvestris Fastigiata Group

Prunus 'Spire' (right)

Prunus 'Umineko'

Pyrus calleryana 'Chanticleer'

Salix exigua

Sorbus 'Autumn Spire'

Taxus baccata 'Fastigiata'

SPREADING

Acer shirasawanum 'Aureum'

Catalpa bignonioides 'Aurea'

Crataegus crus-galli

Ficus carica (right)

Koelreuteria paniculata

Malus floribunda

Morus nigra

Parrotia persica

Prunus 'Shirotae'

Salix integra 'Hakuro-nishiki'

WEEPING

Betula nigra 'Summer Cascade'

Betula pendula 'Youngii' (right)

Cotoneaster 'Hybridus Pendulus'

Fagus sylvatica 'Purpurea Pendula'

Prunus 'Kiku-shidare-zakura'

Pyrus salicifolia 'Pendula'

Salix caprea 'Kilmarnock'

LIGHT CANOPY

Albizia julibrissin f. *rosea* (right)

Alnus glutinosa 'Imperialis'

Aralia elata 'Variegata'

Azara microphylla

Betula pendula

Cornus alternifolia 'Argentea'

Crataegus orientalis

Eucalyptus pauciflora subsp. *niphophila*

Genista aetnensis

Gleditsia triacanthos 'Sunburst'

Prunus × subhirtella 'Autumnalis'

Sorbus aucuparia 'Aspleniifolia'

Tamarix ramosissima

Designing with trees

Trees – or even just one tree – can affect the character of an outdoor space in many different ways. The effect may not be immediate, but the eventual impact of a tree on the look and feel of a garden is quite dramatic, which is why it's important to think carefully about the effect you would like to achieve before deciding what kind of tree to buy and where to plant it.

What trees can do

Planting a tree is frequently the very best way to begin transforming a flat, uninteresting garden. A tree immediately provides height, a focal point, and a sense of scale and enclosure that will influence the garden more and more as time goes by. It won't be long before even a small, young tree takes over from the boundaries as the tallest, most dominant feature in the garden, giving the whole space a new lease of life and a promising future.

It's difficult but very important, at the outset, to visualize the effect that your chosen tree might have in five or ten years' time. A tree's most obvious influence is on the third dimension – height – but you can use trees to manipulate space and change perspective in all kinds of other ways. Think of a tree as a punctuation mark. It can be a full stop at the end of a vista, or create a pause in a path, or lend emphasis by framing an object or a feature. It defines a space and makes it feel more enclosed and secure; it makes a visual link between the garden and the house or other buildings, and helps to anchor other plants such as shrubs or a climber on an arch or pergola. In planning all these effects, the shape of the tree (*see* pages 10–11), will be just as important as its position.

Light and shade

The visual beauty and atmosphere of a garden owe much to light and shade and the different kinds of contrast that are created between them. Trees play a critical and often subtle role in achieving such effects. Areas of light and shade, including dappled shade, can be used to influence the 'flow' of a garden. From a shady place, maybe under a tree, an open sunny space looks warm and appealing, inviting you in the same way as a woodland glade might do. Entering the shade of a tree from an open area can feel mysterious, or perhaps just cool and refreshing. Colour works in a similar way: a tree with silvery leaves or white flowers, especially against a dark background, draws you towards it (particularly at dusk), while trees with dark green or purple foliage tend to recede.

> ### Don't forget
> An important factor in choosing trees is that they must suit the environment in which you plant them – not only the growing conditions (see pages 60–7), but the wider landscape too.

Its elegant form and light-as-air foliage makes *Cornus alternifolia* 'Argentea' a focal point wherever it is planted.

1 *Elaeagnus* 'Quicksilver' (× 1) TREE
2 *Heuchera* 'Purple Petticoats' (× 13)
3 *Anthriscus sylvestris* 'Ravenswing' (× 9)
4 *Juniperus communis* 'Sentinel' (× 4) TREE
5 *Geranium psilostemon* (× 7)
6 *Tulipa* 'Shirley' (× 70)
7 *Allium cristophii* (× 35)

8 *Sedum* 'Matrona' (× 7)
9 *Salvia × superba* (× 6)
10 *Thymus pulegioides* 'Kurt' (× 5)
11 *Pittosporum tenuifolium* 'Tom Thumb' (× 4)
12 *Lavandula angustifolia* 'Hidcote' (× 5)
13 *Nepeta racemosa* 'Walker's Low' (× 4)

14 *Eryngium alpinum* (× 7)
15 *Clematis* 'Étoile Violette' (× 2; trained on trellis)
16 *Pittosporum tenuifolium* 'Purpureum' (× 1) TREE
17 *Cercis siliquastrum* (× 1) TREE
18 *Aquilegia alpina* (× 11)

Trees in borders

Even a single tree gives a border backbone and a focal point, helping to turn what could be a jumble of flowers and foliage into a structured all-year planting scheme. Choose a tree that will contribute positively to the border at more than one time of year, and preferably one that is upright in shape rather than spreading or weeping. Light and delicate silvery foliage, such as that of *Cornus alternifolia* 'Argentea' or

A SUNNY BORDER WITH TREES, SHRUBS AND PERENNIALS (7.5 × 5M/25 × 16FT)

A stepping-stone path curves towards a secluded seat, flanked by a mass of spring and summer colour. Flowers in rich blues and pinks are set off by purple and silver foliage to create a scheme that takes its lead from the flowers and foliage of the Judas tree (*Cercis siliquastrum*) that is the principal feature. Structural evergreens, including junipers and purple pittosporums, give shape to the informal planting.

Elaeagnus 'Quicksilver', is flattering to many other plants. Both these small trees can be pruned to raise their crown above the competition around their feet. Shrubs pruned as trees (*see* page 53) also work well. Columnar trees such as slender

junipers or Irish yews are useful in a different way: for giving your border year-round structure. Or you could choose tightly clipped lollipops or cylinders of box, holly or perhaps beech for their even more formal architectural qualities.

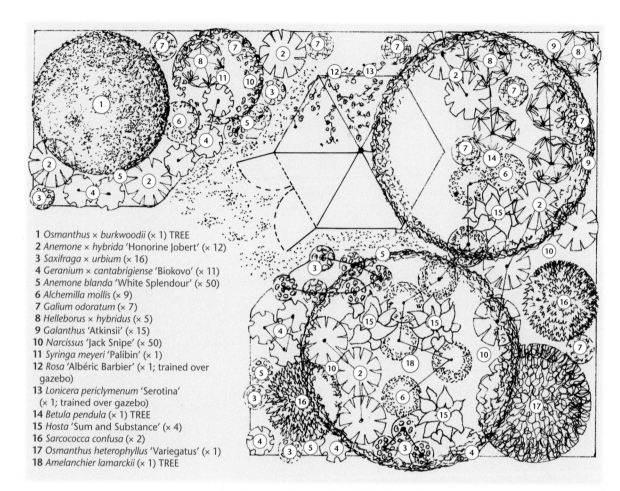

1 *Osmanthus × burkwoodii* (× 1) TREE
2 *Anemone × hybrida* 'Honorine Jobert' (× 12)
3 *Saxifraga × urbium* (× 16)
4 *Geranium × cantabrigiense* 'Biokovo' (× 11)
5 *Anemone blanda* 'White Splendour' (× 50)
6 *Alchemilla mollis* (× 9)
7 *Galium odoratum* (× 7)
8 *Helleborus × hybridus* (× 5)
9 *Galanthus* 'Atkinsii' (× 15)
10 *Narcissus* 'Jack Snipe' (× 50)
11 *Syringa meyeri* 'Palibin' (× 1)
12 *Rosa* 'Albéric Barbier' (× 1; trained over gazebo)
13 *Lonicera periclymenum* 'Serotina' (× 1; trained over gazebo)
14 *Betula pendula* (× 1) TREE
15 *Hosta* 'Sum and Substance' (× 4)
16 *Sarcococca confusa* (× 2)
17 *Osmanthus heterophyllus* 'Variegatus' (× 1)
18 *Amelanchier lamarckii* (× 1) TREE

A woodland area

Woodland-style planting is restful and fresh, especially in spring, and an informal woodland corner can be created even in a small garden with just one or perhaps two trees. Provided their leaf canopies are not too dense, the planting beneath them can be both varied and interesting to look at, as well as easy to maintain. Try to vary the levels of light and shade in the area: if, for example, you use more than one tree, plant each of them as far apart as you can. Include a path, just a

WOODLAND RETREAT WITH GAZEBO OR SUMMERHOUSE 7.5 × 5.5M (25 × 18FT)

Spring fragrance and blossom give way to summer shade in this small garden, with planting that will look fresh and inviting for a long season. Trees partner perennials, bulbs and shrubs in calming greens and whites, and frame a place to sit, sheltered from wind and showers. The layout would also suit a corner of a larger garden.

The fourth dimension

Time is, perhaps, the main factor that makes designing a garden different from designing a building. Once complete, a building stays much the same, but a new garden will look very different after ten years, and it is vital to bear this in mind at the planning stage. The difference over time will be due in no small way to the trees. There's no easy answer to the question of how far ahead you should be thinking when you plant a tree. Some trees grow very slowly, and this may make them appropriate for a small garden. On the other hand, you may not want to wait 25 years for your tree to create an impact. However, never be tempted to plant vigorous, fast-growing varieties of willow and poplar, and certain notorious conifers. Unfortunately, the tree that grows to 3m (10ft) in no time and then, magically, stops growing, has yet to be discovered. *See* page 38 for some slow- and fast-growing trees.

narrow one, to encourage a sense of mystery and adventure, and perhaps a secluded seat. It will be a joy to use on hot summer days, or in spring while there is still plenty of light in which to enjoy the flowers and foliage that will carpet the ground before the leaf canopy appears. This kind of planting is often much more successful under trees than grass, which can struggle without sufficient light or water. Paths can be made of gravel, earth or chipped bark.

Trees as specimens

A tree chosen as a specimen (to stand alone as a feature), whether for a lawn, a patio or perhaps a front garden, commands a lot of attention and needs to have sculptural qualities as well as a long season of (preferably) changing interest. Size

Do your homework!

If you want to gauge the appearance, size and effect of a particular tree at maturity, there's no substitute for seeing one 'in the flesh' before you buy. Visiting parks and gardens that are open to the public, whether regularly or occasionally through the National Gardens Scheme, can be an inspiring and instructive way to get to know trees at first hand. In some, such as botanic gardens and arboretums, the trees will be labelled. Elsewhere you may be able to talk to gardeners who have grown and lived with them – an invaluable aid to sorting the sheep from the goats when it comes to assessing particular trees. Some helpful nurseries and tree growers also maintain a small garden or arboretum with mature specimens to help you compare and choose.

Don't forget

Spare a thought for your neighbours' gardens, as well as your own, when you are choosing a spot for a tree. Consider where its shade will fall when it is mature. If it is likely to plunge next door's patio into gloom, think again.

With its pretty, silver foliage, the popular weeping pear *Pyrus salicifolia* 'Pendula' can make a good lawn specimen, especially if it is kept pruned to shape as it ages.

is significant, too: it must neither dwarf the rest of a garden, nor be so small that it looks out of scale. If it is visible from indoors, winter interest will be important: this might be an attractive branch structure, like that of a birch, or a feature such as the handsome bark of *Acer griseum* or *Betula utilis* var. *jacquemontii* 'Grayswood Ghost'. Flowers could be a priority, but choose something out of the ordinary, and a tree that

has unusual foliage or fruits at a different season from most others: *Cercis siliquastrum* or *Davidia involucrata* perhaps, rather than a flowering cherry like everyone else's!

Don't forget

Practicalities are important as well as looks. Don't place a thorny tree near a path or play area. If you want to eat under a tree, avoid any that drop messy fruit or may be full of wasps or aphids – such as mulberries, plums and limes.

| # Trees for containers

Trees grown in containers have a variety of useful and attractive roles to play, in all sorts of gardens – not just small ones. An appropriate tree in the right container can set the tone and style of a particular area of the garden and give a sense of scale and enclosure to a patio or other seating area. It can also be a formal counterpoint to exuberant border planting. On a practical level, a potted tree can be positioned to give screening or shade where it is needed – a good solution in paved areas where a tree cannot be planted in the ground.

Wind-resistant *Arbutus unedo*, a good roof-garden tree for mild areas.

Choosing containers

A tree in a container is sure to be a focal point in the garden, so it's important to choose the plant and its container together, to reflect the particular style you are aiming for: formal, contemporary, oriental or 'cottagey', for example. A simple tree such as clipped bay or box might be best partnered by a pot with some sort of pattern, while a more decorative tree – one with variegated or intricately shaped foliage, for instance – will have more impact in a plain container. There are practical considerations, too. Any tree in a pot can easily become top-heavy, so whatever the style of your container, make sure it is large and heavy enough to make the whole thing stable. Tall, narrow containers are less stable than ones with a large footprint and a squat shape, such as a half-barrel. Remember that if you plant a tree in an urn-shaped or other narrow-necked container, it will be difficult or impossible to get the tree out for repotting without breaking the pot. Ceramic pots should be frost proof and sturdy enough not to crack or break easily as the tree's roots grow.

Caring for trees in containers

With stability in mind, it's a good idea to use a loam-based (soil-based) compost for trees in pots: John Innes No. 3 is ideal. Loam-based composts are heavier, settle firmly around roots, and retain water and nutrients well.

Pruning trees in containers

A tree in a container tends to draw the eye, so make sure that it is always kept looking its best. Remove dying or discoloured leaves and cut off damaged or dead twigs promptly. Most deciduous trees look better and stay healthier if they are pruned for shape from time to time, removing crossing or overcrowded branches and keeping the crown of the tree open. If trees in containers need to be pruned to keep them compact, crown reduction is a useful technique that works with most species. Some, such as willows or *Acer negundo*, lend themselves to pollarding. *See* pages 50–1 for pruning techniques.

Don't forget

Choose a sheltered spot for trees in containers. When they are in leaf, it's easy for the crown of the tree to act like a sail on breezy days and make the whole thing overbalance. If your garden is very windy, it's probably best to have your trees planted firmly in the ground.

Well-kept potted specimens of sweet bay are a year-round asset to a garden.

Conifers in containers

If you take care to choose slow-growing varieties, conifers make good trees for containers. They contribute all-year structure and are an excellent foil for other container plants; quite a number of them, such as compact junipers, cypresses and pines (shown below is *Pinus mugo* 'Carsten's Wintergold'), are also reasonably drought-tolerant and undemanding in terms of feeding and routine care.

Remember to use ericaceous compost if the tree dislikes lime and prefers acid soil. Young trees should be repotted into a slightly larger container every few years as they grow. However, once tree and container reach a certain size, repotting becomes an unwieldy task and it is much easier to refresh the compost in the pot every year or two by removing the top layer (about 5cm/2in) and replacing it with fresh compost into which you've mixed a little slow-release fertilizer.

The single most important thing to remember for trees in pots is water. Trees with confined roots do not have the reserves of those planted in the open ground and drying out can quite easily kill them. Water in the evening so that the tree can take up water overnight, and consider moving the pot to a cooler position in summer.

Trees in pots will benefit from a liquid feed once a month or so.

Young trees in containers will probably need staking just as they would in the ground, at least until the trunk is thick and strong enough to support the tree without help. Set a short stake in the pot to its full depth when you plant the tree, as close to the trunk as you can without disturbing the rootball, and use a purpose-made tree tie to fix the tree to the stake.

Choosing trees for containers

Be sure to choose a tree that looks good for a long season, especially if it is on a patio where it will be visible from the house in winter. Attractive foliage is pretty well essential, and if you choose a tree for its flowers or fruit, make sure that it has worthwhile features at other times of year too. For ideas for trees for containers *see* page 39, and for advice on growing fruit trees in pots *see* pages 14–15.

A tree in a pot doesn't have to be a long-term feature – as it would be if it were planted in the garden – and one of the advantages of container growing is that you can ring the changes. Some trees are attractive when young but may start to lose their looks in the longer term: these can be ideal for containers, for a few years. Examples include *Cryptomeria japonica* Elegans Group – small trees or shrubs with soft green, feathery foliage that changes to purplish bronze in winter – or the attractive and easy but rather invasive *Rhus typhina*, whose habit of throwing out runners, or suckers, from its base is not a problem in a pot. Other trees are grown for their novelty value, such as the twisted willow (*Salix babylonica* var. *pekinensis* 'Tortuosa') and the corkscrew hazel (*Corylus avellana* 'Contorta'). Plant trees like these in a container and you can enjoy their quirkiness for a few years, then give them away and grow something different.

Use containers to control growth habit.
① The variegated sycamore *Acer pseudoplatanus* 'Esk Sunset' can be kept compact in a pot.
② *Rhus typhina* can't sucker among other plants.

Trees as planting partners

We tend not to think very much about the space under and around trees. Too often it is given over to poor, thin grass, or plants that are clearly struggling. It's a pity to waste this valuable space, especially in a small garden. A partnership of trees with other plants can make a really memorable picture: think of a bluebell wood, a spring orchard or a Mediterranean olive grove full of wildflowers. With suitable plants and an imaginative approach, it's quite easy to plan a scheme that will do justice to both the tree and its companions.

Planting under trees

The space underneath an established tree will seldom offer ideal planting conditions. Trees make considerable demands on the soil, and some have shallow roots that don't leave much food or water for anything else. Others, such as beeches and conifers, have a dense canopy that deflects rainfall from the roots and casts very deep shade: it's hard to grow very much under a beech, for instance, or beneath many conifers and other evergreens, for example cherry laurel (*Prunus laurocerasus*).

The first step towards overcoming these problems is to make the soil and situation better, and the second involves deciding on the effect you would like, and then choosing plants to help you achieve it.

Improving the soil is an obvious starting point. Mulch over a large circle underneath the tree's canopy with well-rotted compost. The tree itself will respond gratefully to this and, if you do it in early spring, when the ground is damp, you should find that it's reasonably easy to make planting holes come the autumn, which is the best time to plant beneath trees. By then, branches will soon be bare and winter rainfall will penetrate the ground beneath.

Pruning to thin or raise the crown, or canopy, of a mature tree (*see* page 51) is a useful tactic for improving planting possibilities. With more light, air and water available, a wider range of plants is likely to thrive.

Bulbs under trees

In many respects, spring bulbs are obvious partners for deciduous trees. It is fairly easy to tuck them into small holes among tree roots,

and they complete their growth cycle before the tree comes into leaf, making the most of the early-spring sunshine and rainfall. Then they simply become dormant and make no competing demands on the soil in summer. In their first year, at least, poor soil is not a problem for bulbs, and if you have improved the soil under the tree – and, perhaps, added a handful or two of slow-release fertilizer or a bucketful of compost – many bulbs should be able to replenish their reserves and carry on flowering in future years. Daffodils, so often seen under trees, aren't always the best bulbs to choose as they are quite demanding of moisture, and their large leaves can look really very untidy after flowering. Instead, try small, tough spring bulbs such as snowdrops, *Crocus tommasinianus*, *Scilla* and *Chionodoxa*, or hardy cyclamen corms, which are tolerant of both drought and shade and give two seasons of interest with their dainty, swept-back flowers and long-lasting marbled foliage.

A carpet of bulbs can be a perfect foil for a spring-blossoming tree, such as a flowering cherry or a crab apple. A little forethought is needed to ensure a harmonious picture and simultaneous flowering, though. Neither a magnolia in all its glory rising from a mass of dying snowdrop foliage, nor a cloud of

The late-summer and autumn flowers of *Cyclamen hederifolium* are a welcome surprise under trees, just when many other plants are beginning to look tired.

> **Don't forget**
>
> Don't expect the same plants to thrive on the sunny south side of a tree as on the shadier north side. Different plants will thrive in the differing light conditions – though all will need to be reasonably drought-tolerant.

delicate pink blossom hovering over several dozen stridently yellow daffodils, make attractive or successful combinations. Get to know what is likely to flower with what, and buy bulbs accordingly. Small blue or white bulbs, such as *Anemone blanda* and its cultivar 'White Splendour', look fresh and pretty beneath just about any tree, and they die off unobtrusively. Yellow-and-white narcissi under a white-flowered pear or plum can really capture the essence of spring – but try to include other plants that will grow up and mask their untidy dying leaves.

Perennials under trees

A carpet of flowering perennials makes the ideal underplanting for trees. Their expanding foliage arrives just in time to take over from fading spring bulbs, with flowers to look forward to when fresh spring colours

Acer griseum underplanted with hardy geraniums and self-seeding Welsh poppies – an ideal combination to take over from fading spring bulbs in dappled shade.

Ferns

Ferns are magical plants, especially in spring when they unfurl their strange, fiddle-like necks and evoke something of the atmosphere of a primeval swamp. Many are ideal woodland plants: perfect companions for trees and tolerant of shade. If they are happy, a minute percentage of the dust-like spores they shed will develop rather excitingly into infant new plants, often appearing in the most unlikely places, where you would not have thought to plant anything.

Common polypody (*Polypodium vulgare*) is a good, tough fern to begin with. It is evergreen, and happy in dry situations, as is the soft shield fern (*Polystichum setiferum*), another native with many intriguing frilly cultivars. Larger and more dramatic, but equally long-suffering, is the male fern (*Dryopteris filix-mas*). A lovely fern for damper soil in semi-shade is the ostrich, or shuttlecock, fern (*Matteuccia struthiopteris*), with statuesque fronds up to 1.2m (4ft) high.

are on the wane. Keeping the ground covered with foliage does the tree a good turn too, preventing evaporation and smothering weeds. Aim to create a tapestry effect using perennials that have good foliage, so you keep up the interest before and after flowering. If you are choosing companions for a newly planted tree

you can be a bit adventurous, but under a mature tree that has taken its toll on the soil it may be better to stick to the old die-hards that have tough, drought-tolerant roots: try epimediums, pulmonarias, brunneras and hardy geraniums.

Geranium macrorrhizum has to be one of the most indestructible hardy geraniums. It quickly forms a weed-suppressing, flowery mat in the most unpromising conditions. It does have a rather pungent smell, which some people dislike. If you aren't among them, a good one to try is *Geranium macrorrhizum* 'Spessart' – its flowers are white with a hint of pink. Other hardy geraniums for shady places include *Geranium sylvaticum* 'Album' or any of the many cultivars of *Geranium phaeum*. The dark-flowered types are the most sought after, but in shade beneath trees it is pale flowers that show up best, for example white *Geranium phaeum* 'Album'. Sweet woodruff (*Galium odoratum*) makes a weed-smothering carpet with its delicate foliage and masses of tiny,

dainty white flowers – but it can be invasive if the soil is at all rich.

For something larger and more dramatic, go for *Geranium psilostemon*, a vigorous hardy geranium with black-eyed magenta flowers. These are perfect partners for another familiar and tough perennial, *Alchemilla mollis,* with its shapely leaves and fresh lime-yellow flowers. Euphorbias are also unbeatable for freshness. Many prefer sun to shade, but a cultivar of the native wood spurge, *Euphorbia amygdaloides* var. *robbiae*, will thrive in both. It looks its best in dappled shade, unfurling its flowerheads in early spring and then reflecting every available ray of light from its dazzling lime-green bracts. It

is inclined to run rather, but is a useful and attractive plant for inhospitable places where little else will grow.

Shrubs with trees

There's no denying that evergreen shrubs can hide a multitude of sins, and several compact, shade-tolerant ones are adept at coping with life

Where the ground is not too dry and shady, hydrangeas can make colourful late-summer partners for trees.

in the shade of trees, helping to keep the tree roots covered and adding interest near to ground level. Make the most of limited space by choosing such shrubs for their own sake, not merely as a foil for the tree.

A shrub like *Sarcococca confusa* is undemanding and has healthy-looking greenery, but it also offers winter flowers with a lovely fragrance; *Cotoneaster dammeri* makes efficient ground cover but also brightens dull days and pleases birdlife with its abundant red berries. Another tough customer is *Mahonia aquifolium*. It can survive almost anywhere, but its glossy leaves and bright yellow spring flowers will look all the better for an annual mulch of well-rotted compost.

A number of native evergreen shrubs will grow happily beneath trees, including holly, box and yew (*see* page 19). These are garden stalwarts, but sometimes it's good to be a bit more adventurous. More unusual low-growing native evergreen shrubs that tolerate quite deep shade are the wonderfully fragrant spurge laurel (*Daphne laureola*) and butcher's broom (*Ruscus aculeatus*), a spiny little shrub with amazingly large, long-lasting, bright red berries. Self-fertile forms are now available, which means that you don't need to have both a male and a female to be sure of getting berries on your plant.

Golden catalpa makes a handsome host tree for almost any clematis that has flowers in dark, rich colours.

A heady late-spring partnership: the honeysuckle *Lonicera × italica* blooms at the same time as hawthorn.

Climbers with trees

In gardens there's a tendency to grow climbers against walls. They can look marvellous if they are properly pruned and tied in, but there's an easier option, which replicates the way many of them grow in the wild. There they clamber up through other plants, such as trees, that give them support. A climber growing up a tree works particularly well where space is at a premium because it offers a second season of interest to, say, a tree that flowers in spring, or one whose autumn colour is its chief claim to fame.

With their twining, self-clinging tendrils, clematis are ideal for this role. They may take a while to establish, but once they have got their roots down they will appreciate the shade of the tree's canopy yet enjoy scrambling up towards the light to flower. *Clematis* 'Étoile Violette' is a reliable choice for a

larger tree: its purple flowers look especially good against the pale leaves of *Sorbus aria* 'Lutescens', while a tree with dark foliage is the perfect foil for the mauve-pink blooms of *Clematis* 'Comtesse de Bouchaud'. Both clematis are late-flowering and can be cut hard back in late winter, giving the crown of the host tree a chance to shed its load once a year. Other climbers to try with trees include rambling roses that are not too vigorous, such as 'Albéric Barbier' (creamy-white, scented flowers), and fragrant honeysuckles such as *Lonicera periclymenum* 'Graham Thomas'.

Any climber destined to clamber up a tree should be planted a little way from the tree trunk to give it the best chance of survival. Make its hole as large as you can, with generous helpings of compost, and train it up into the canopy on canes or wire. Keep it well watered for at least the first year.

Don't forget

If you are growing a climber through a tree, make sure the two are evenly matched. A scrambler like *Clematis montana* would swamp a young rowan, for example, while one of the compact varieties of clematis such as 'Petit Faucon' would be lost in a big old apple tree.

Trees for a purpose

Choosing a tree for specific conditions, effects or purposes need not be daunting. These lists, offering a limited selection of the best small garden trees, will help you find the right one for the job. For more ideas, *see* pages 19, 22, 53 and 64–7, the Design palette on pages 26–7 and the A–Z directory on pages 69–91.

Cercis siliquastrum – an unusual special feature, dazzling in flower.

Best fast-growing trees

Acer campestre
Alnus glutinosa 'Imperialis'
Betula pendula
Corylus avellana
Cotoneaster frigidus 'Cornubia'
Elaeagnus angustifolia
Eucalyptus gunnii
Genista aetnensis
Gleditsia triacanthos 'Sunburst'
Malus hupehensis
Olea europaea
Sorbus 'Joseph Rock'

Best for screening

Acer campestre
Arbutus unedo
Betula pendula
Carpinus caroliniana
Crataegus × *lavalleei* 'Carrierei'
Eucalyptus pauciflora subsp. *niphophila*
Prunus cerasifera
Prunus lusitanica
Pyrus salicifolia 'Pendula'
Sorbus hupehensis

Best for sitting under

Betula pendula
Catalpa bignonioides 'Aurea'
Koelreuteria paniculata
Malus domestica
Prunus 'Shizuka'
Sorbus aucuparia
Syringa vulgaris

Best evergreen trees

Abies koreana
Buxus sempervirens
Cupressus sempervirens
Eucalyptus pauciflora subsp. *niphophila*
Ilex aquifolium
Laurus nobilis
Ligustrum lucidum 'Excelsum Superbum'
Osmanthus × *burkwoodii*
Photinia × *fraseri* 'Red Robin'
Pinus sylvestris Fastigiata Group
Pittosporum tenuifolium
Prunus lusitanica
Taxus baccata 'Fastigiata'

Best for keeping small by pruning

Acer negundo 'Flamingo'
Buxus sempervirens
Corylus avellana
Ilex aquifolium
Laurus nobilis
Photinia × *fraseri* 'Red Robin'
Prunus lusitanica
Salix integra 'Hakuro-nishiki'

Best for topiary

Buxus sempervirens
Ilex aquifolium
Ilex crenata
Laurus nobilis
Phillyrea angustifolia
Prunus lusitanica
Pyrus salicifolia 'Pendula'
Taxus baccata

Best for all-year interest

Betula pendula
Crataegus × *lavalleei* 'Carrierei'
Cryptomeria japonica Elegans Group
Ilex aquifolium
Sorbus cashmiriana
Stewartia pseudocamellia

Best slow-growing trees

Acer griseum
Aesculus × *carnea* 'Briotii'
Cornus controversa 'Variegata'
Davidia involucrata
Morus nigra
Parrotia persica

Best for a dainty effect

Acacia baileyana 'Purpurea'
Acer palmatum 'Crippsii'
Acer palmatum 'Trompenburg'
Albizia julibrissin f. rosea
Cercis canadensis 'Forest Pansy'
Cornus alternifolia 'Argentea'
Prunus × subhirtella 'Autumnalis'
Robinia × slavinii 'Hillieri'
Salix integra 'Hakuro-nishiki'
Sorbus cashmiriana
Sorbus vilmorinii

Best for rural gardens

Acer campestre
Alnus glutinosa
Betula pendula
Corylus avellana
Ilex aquifolium
Malus domestica
Malus hupehensis
Prunus cerasifera
Sorbus aucuparia
Taxus baccata

Best for urban gardens

Acer palmatum 'Bloodgood'
Acer palmatum 'Osakazuki'
Catalpa bignonioides 'Aurea'
Crataegus × lavalleei 'Carrierei'
Ilex aquifolium
Juniperus chinensis 'Aurea'
Ligustrum lucidum 'Excelsum Superbum'
Magnolia 'Heaven Scent'
Prunus lusitanica
Pyrus calleryana 'Chanticleer'

Most pollution-tolerant

Betula pendula
Crataegus × lavalleei 'Carrierei'
Fagus sylvatica 'Dawyck'
Ilex aquifolium
Prunus lusitanica
Pyrus calleryana 'Chanticleer'

Best for courtyards

Acacia baileyana 'Purpurea'
Acer negundo 'Flamingo'
Albizia julibrissin f. rosea
Buxus sempervirens
Cercis canadensis 'Forest Pansy'
Drimys winteri
Juniperus communis 'Hibernica'
Laurus nobilis
Osmanthus delavayi
Robinia × slavinii 'Hillieri'
Salix integra 'Hakuro-nishiki'
Sorbus 'Autumn Spire'
Taxus baccata 'Fastigiata'

Best for containers

Acer negundo (pollarded)
Acer palmatum 'Beni-maiko'
Albizia julibrissin f. rosea
Cordyline australis
Cotoneaster 'Hybridus Pendulus'
Ilex crenata 'Fastigiata'
Juniperus communis 'Hibernica'
Laurus nobilis
Olea europaea
Prunus incisa 'Kojo-no-mai'
Salix caprea 'Kilmarnock'
Sorbus koehneana
Trachycarpus fortunei

Best for a special feature

Arbutus unedo 'Atlantic'
Cercis siliquastrum
Cryptomeria japonica Elegans Group
Cydonia oblonga
Fagus sylvatica 'Purpurea Pendula'
Genista aetnensis
Hibiscus syriacus
Koelreuteria paniculata
Magnolia salicifolia 'Wada's Memory'
Mespilus germanica
Morus nigra
Parrotia persica
Prunus cerasus 'Morello'
Ulmus × hollandica 'Dampieri Aurea'

Best for fragrance

Azara microphylla
Clerodendrum trichotomum var. fargesii
Cydonia oblonga
Drimys winteri
Elaeagnus 'Quicksilver'
Eucryphia × nymansensis 'Nymansay'
Hoheria sexstylosa
Ligustrum lucidum 'Excelsum Superbum'
Osmanthus × burkwoodii
Pittosporum tenuifolium
Prunus 'Shizuka'
Syringa vulgaris

Best for edible fruit and nuts

Corylus avellana (hazelnut)
Cydonia oblonga (quince)
Malus domestica (apple)
Mespilus germanica (medlar)
Morus nigra (black mulberry)
Olea europaea (olive)
Prunus armeniaca (apricot)
Prunus avium (sweet cherry)
Prunus cerasus 'Morello' (Morello cherry)
Prunus domestica (plum)
Prunus dulcis (almond)
Prunus insititia (damson)
Prunus persica (peach/nectarine)
Pyrus communis (pear)

Something different ...

Aesculus pavia
Clerodendrum trichotomum var. fargesii
Cornus kousa var. chinensis
Crinodendron hookerianum
Davidia involucrata
Embothrium coccineum
Halesia monticola
Hoheria sexstylosa 'Stardust'
Luma apiculata
Magnolia kobus
Nyssa sinensis
Stewartia pseudocamellia
Styrax japonicus

Planting and growing

A well-chosen tree in the right place is an immeasurable asset to a garden, giving years of pleasure, every day, for relatively low input – provided you take a little trouble in the early stages. Think carefully about the positioning of your tree and spend a bit of time choosing the right variety and selecting a healthy, well-shaped specimen. Enjoy making a good job of the planting, and follow up with regular checks on the tree's wellbeing. You're starting something that could enhance the garden for generations.

Where to plant a tree

At least two considerations should drive the process of deciding where to plant a tree. First, think about the visual impact – how the tree will look and how it will affect its surroundings (*see* pages 28–31). Second, take into account the practicalities. The tree must have space and light to grow, over the longer term, without disturbing or damaging nearby buildings or any landscaping features, and (at least as important) it must have a good environment below ground to accommodate its expanding root system.

What's under the ground?

It's easy to ignore this simple but important question until you've bought your tree and begin to dig the hole only to get an unwelcome surprise in the form of a drain or your gas main. Try to establish the location of any underground services before you decide where to plant the tree: inadvertently chopping a cable with a spade, or distorting a pipe when the tree roots begin to grow, could have quite dangerous consequences. You may be lucky enough to have a plan that shows where services run, but if not then a little detective work based on the location of inspection covers, and outlets where cables or pipes leave the house, may well give you some useful clues.

Trees and buildings

Everyone knows that trees should not be planted too near to buildings, but how close is too close? Unfortunately there's no clear-cut answer because the way the tree will affect the ground around the building depends on several variables, such as the tree's vigour and growth habit, and the nature of the soil. But as a very rough rule of thumb that would apply to most types of ornamental garden tree, the planting hole should be at least as far from the building as the expected height of the mature tree. Avoid trees with vigorous roots – willows and poplars are among the worst offenders – if buildings or drains are anywhere near.

It's got too big ...

Overgrown conifers can be a serious problem in gardens, eventually cutting out light all year round and, if they become unstable, even threatening buildings. Most conifers, including monkey-puzzles and 'rescued' Christmas trees, are completely unsuitable for small plots, yet you see them in gardens everywhere. Even hedging can be problematic: a hedge of × *Cuprocyparis leylandii* near a building may seem fine while it is regularly maintained, but a change of circumstances or ownership can result in neglect and before you know it the hedge that was planted in good faith becomes a row of trees higher than the house. With posterity in mind, it is better to avoid planting anything at all vigorous near a building.

The trees here frame the path and terrace, but are wisely planted at a safe distance from the house.

Choosing and buying trees

A tree is one of the most significant garden investments you will make: it is a purchase that is important to get right because with luck it will be part of your life for many years. Take time to choose a tree that not only appeals to you but also will be happy in the conditions you can offer (*see* pages 38–9 and 60–91 for suggestions and guidance). But the decision-making process doesn't end with selecting the type of tree. There are also the questions where, what size, and in what form to buy it.

Bare-root, container-grown or rootballed?

There is a long tradition of trees being supplied as bare-root, dormant plants between late autumn and early spring, and this is still a good way to buy them. Bare-root trees tend to be deciduous. They are usually cheaper, easier to transport, and often gain a firmer roothold than container-grown specimens. The trees are grown in the nursery's fields, where an annual 'undercutting' of the root system prepares them for lifting, with minimal damage, when they are old enough to sell. This process encourages the trees to form a compact and shallow root system that will be able to withstand later transplanting more easily.

Buying a bare-root tree will probably mean a winter expedition to a specialist tree nursery, but this can be a pleasure in itself, and a source of invaluable advice from people who really know their trees. The choice of both varieties and sizes is likely to be wider at a nursery than in a garden centre. Many nurseries also sell bare-root trees online; the advantages are the same, with the important exception that you can't see what you are buying or choose the specimen you like best. Some varieties, including birch, may not succeed when transplanted bare-root; if transplanted from the open ground, they will often be rootballed.

Rootballed trees

Many nurseries sell evergreens such as hollies and yews, and certain deciduous trees, as rootballed plants. They are lifted from the nursery field during the winter, and the ball of soil around their roots is

Yews are often sold as rootballed trees. The net wrapping keeps their young fibrous roots in contact with the soil.

wrapped in a permeable material such as hessian (or sometimes encased in wire mesh) to keep it in place. This helps protect the roots from the shock of being transplanted. Rootballed trees come with a lot of earth and can be very heavy; lift the tree from the base, and get help if necessary.

Container-grown trees

Most trees sold in garden centres are pot-grown, usually in 15-litre containers. Being established in a container of soil gives the tree a 'shelf life', and this means you can see it in full leaf and, in theory, plant it at any time. You will need to be fussy when choosing, though. A container-grown tree that has been in its pot for too long is no bargain, however cheap. It may have become starved of nutrients, or the roots may have curled round the inside of the pot. Once in the ground, constricted roots will find it hard to spread out and give the tree the firm roothold it needs. A container-grown tree in prime condition, however, is likely to be a good investment.

Large specimens

A growing demand for instant gardens has boosted sales of large specimen trees in containers up to 1,500 litres in size. Trade nurseries once sold these exclusively to professionals for big landscaping projects, but they are increasingly

Choosing a container-grown tree at a garden centre offers the advantage that you can buy your tree in leaf and see exactly what you are getting.

Nursery tree sizes

Tree nurseries have a traditional system of specifying the sizes of their trees.

■ Trees up to 2.4m (8ft) tall are graded by height, in increments of 30cm. So a tree labelled '180–210' is between 180 and 210cm (6–7ft) tall.

■ Trees over 2.4m (8ft) are classified by girth – the circumference of the stem at 1m (40in) above ground level. (For conifers and multi-stemmed trees, *see* below.) A 'standard' tree has a clear stem of at least 1.8m (6ft). As a convenient and simple rule of thumb: the girth in centimetres roughly corresponds to the height in feet. So a 'standard' tree, with a girth of 8–10cm, is about 8–10ft (2.5–3m) tall; a 'heavy standard', with a girth of 12–14cm, is about 12–14ft (3.7–4.3m) tall. Generally, a tree one size larger is one year older.

■ Conifers and multi-stemmed trees are graded by height in increments of 50cm, for example '350–400' (11–13ft tall).

■ Trees referred to as large specimens are 8–9m (26–30ft) tall and have a girth of 40cm (16in) or more.

finding favour with gardeners too. Such trees do make a quick impact, but there are disadvantages – not only the price (which can be hair-raising, even without the heavy lifting equipment needed to move and plant the largest specimens), but also the sheer unwieldiness of a tree that comes in a huge, heavy pot and is nearly as tall as your house. In some cases, larger trees can also be slow to establish and, within four or five years, a small specimen of a fast-growing subject may well overtake a larger one planted at the same time. And, while a young tree may not give instant gratification, you can enjoy the old-fashioned pleasure of watching it grow and mature year by year – safe in the knowledge that it hasn't broken the bank.

Cercis canadensis 'Forest Pansy' – a rather delicate beauty, best pot-grown to minimize transplanting stress.

Tools and equipment

As well as the usual planting and weeding tools, a basic kit of secateurs, saw and a pair of loppers will enable you to tackle most of the tree work that needs to be done in a small to medium-sized garden. If you tried, maybe you could find uses for other equipment, but there's a lot to be said for buying a minimum of good-quality equipment and keeping things simple. For any drastic tree surgery, you need to call in the professionals.

Secateurs

A good pair of secateurs, well maintained to keep them sharp and clean, will make short work of cutting any woody stems up to about 1cm (½in) thick. Choose between bypass secateurs, which work like scissors (and are good for brittle stems), and anvil secateurs, which operate more like a knife cutting down onto a flat surface. Specialist suppliers make secateurs for left-handed gardeners, and ones with swivel handles that help prevent blisters and aching hands after a prolonged pruning session. A purpose-made leather holster attached to a belt keeps your secateurs handy and safe when you don't want them in your hand.

You don't need many tools for the routine tree-pruning jobs, and for anything more demanding it's always best to employ a tree surgeon.

Loppers

Loppers work like giant secateurs, with stout blades and long handles to give extra leverage for cutting thicker branches, up to about 2.5cm (1in) in diameter. Some have telescopic handles that can be extended to reach high branches; another modification is a ratchet system to enable you to cut in several gentle stages using less pressure. Only buy loppers that feel sturdy and strong, because cutting thick branches exerts considerable force on them.

Saws

You will need a saw to cut through anything that is more than about 2.5cm (1in) thick. A narrow-bladed pruning saw is a useful item for getting into awkward angles. One with a blade that folds away into the handle is convenient and safe to tuck into a pocket. Most pruning saws cut on the 'pull' stroke, which makes them easy to manipulate, though for heavy work a bow saw is more effective. This consists of a replaceable blade with coarse teeth, held taut in a sprung metal frame. The smallest size is likely to be adequate for most garden work.

Gloves

A pair of stout leather gloves or gauntlets is useful for all tree-pruning jobs, helping to protect your hands and wrists from cuts and scratches, and providing a better grip on both tools and plants. Make sure they fit well so that you can feel what you are doing: gloves that are too large can be a liability. Thermal-lined gloves are great for winter pruning – worth every penny on a crisp, frosty day.

Don't forget

Prune only with clean tools. Diseases can very easily spread from plant to plant via pruning equipment. Use a proprietary garden disinfectant to clean cutting tools after you have used them on any diseased trees. Keep blades free of dried sap and other deposits by rubbing them occasionally with fine sandpaper or wire wool.

Planting a tree

The big decisions as to what tree to plant, and where to buy it and plant it, are just the start of the process. Good soil preparation before planting, and secure staking, will then give your tree the best possible chance in life – followed up with conscientious aftercare, especially for the vital first year or two.

When to plant

With container-grown trees widely available, it is possible to plant at any time of year, but to maximize your tree's chances of success and to minimize the work involved, the counsel of perfection is probably late autumn. This is also a good time for bare-root trees, which must be planted while dormant. Nursery availability will be at its peak in autumn, especially with bare-root stock, so the choice will be wide: leave it until March and you may be left with the trees no-one else wanted. Autumn planting gives the tree several months to settle in before it begins to grow and take up water in significant amounts. In late autumn there will be residual warmth in the soil to get the tree off to a good start, little risk of severe frost in its early days, and little likelihood of drought.

Preparation and planting

Experts have long been aware that trees fare badly in compacted ground. Even very old trees can be rejuvenated simply by aerating the surrounding soil to allow the roots a free run, and the same applies to newly planted trees. So, whatever the condition of your soil, it is important to dig over a wide area around where the tree is to go, breaking up the soil and adding organic matter to help it hold moisture. This will be much more effective than planting into a small hole full of good soil, from which the roots may find it hard to escape.

The hole for the tree should be three to four times as wide as the rootball and a little deeper. Some experts now prefer a square hole to a round one as the roots are less likely to grow in a spiral.

The planting depth of the tree within the hole is important too. Sit the tree in the base of the hole and if necessary add a mound of soil below the rootball to bring the tree up to the right height. The surface of the soil, including any layer of mulch on top, should be level with the 'root flare': this is the point where the trunk thickens slightly just above the topmost roots. It should correspond to the mark made by the soil on the trunk of a nursery-grown tree. Planting more deeply could cause the base of the trunk to rot, while shallower planting may leave roots exposed once the soil settles. When the hole is filled, create a shallow saucer around the trunk so that water will drain directly down to the tree's roots.

Tree supports

Newly planted trees need support for their first year or two to keep them anchored in the ground. Freshly settled roots are easily disturbed as the tree flexes with the wind, and effective staking can help prevent this. It is vital that the stakes or stake should be stout and driven firmly into the ground, or the tree can end up supporting the stake!

The best methods of staking trees are hotly debated among experts, but the general consensus is that the crown of the tree should be free to move naturally in the wind. This

Tree stakes

There are various ways to support a tree. These are some commonly used methods.

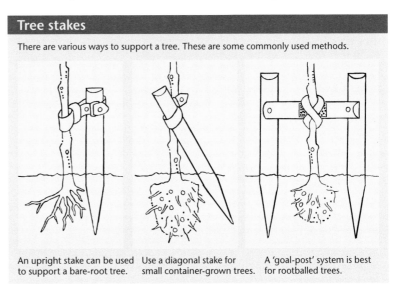

An upright stake can be used to support a bare-root tree.

Use a diagonal stake for small container-grown trees.

A 'goal-post' system is best for rootballed trees.

A young tree like this *Malus floribunda* will benefit from having a circle around its base kept clear of competing grass and weeds for the first few years.

Staking small and bare-root trees

Small and bare-root trees are normally supported with a sturdy, upright stake next to the trunk. Drive it into the appropriate part of the hole before the tree is planted.

Staking container-grown and rootballed trees

For a small container-grown tree, use a diagonal stake, driven into the ground at a 45-degree angle with the top facing into the prevailing wind. For larger trees, use two vertical stakes (or even three, in a triangle), driven into the ground just beyond the rootball. Fit each with a flexible tie that passes around the trunk and holds it gently in place.

For rootballed trees and large container-grown specimens, make a 'goal post' with two stakes, up to 1m (40in) high, one on either side of the tree, and a cross-beam onto which the tree is secured with cushioning tree ties.

Water, water

Tree roots should never be allowed to dry out. A dormant bare-root tree should be kept temporarily wrapped in a slightly damp material such as sacking, and if conditions are

means that the trunk, if it is fairly sturdy, should be supported about 60cm (2ft) from the ground rather than at the top of it. Secure the tree to the stake with a purpose-made, adjustable tree tie fitted with a protective buffer to prevent the tree rubbing against the stake. Fix the tie to the stake with a nail (some ties have a hole for this) so it won't slip.

Magic mycorrhizae

Experts now have a better understanding of the complex relationships between plants and potentially beneficial mycorrhizal fungi that live in the soil and colonize plant roots. These boost a plant's ability to absorb nutrients and water, helping the plant to establish and thrive. Mycorrhizal preparations in powder form are now readily available and seem to be proving very beneficial for newly planted trees and shrubs.

Don't forget

As the tree grows, remember to make a regular check on the ties, stakes and any guards you may be using to ensure that everything is still doing its job properly.

unsuitable for planting within a day or two, the tree should be 'heeled in': dig a shallow hole for the rootball and keep it covered with soil until you are able to plant the tree in its permanent home.

A good soak for an hour in a bucket of water before planting will stand container-grown and bare-root trees in good stead. After planting, water to help settle the soil around the roots with no air gaps. And don't assume you can then abandon the watering can. Throughout its first growing season the tree will need thorough watering as soon as the soil begins to dry out. Enough water to fill a standard watering can (10 litres/2 gallons) once or twice a week is much better than a daily sprinkling, which encourages the roots to come up to the surface.

Keep the ground around the newly planted tree clear of grass and weeds for at least the first two or three growing seasons. A circle about 1m (40in) in diameter should be large enough to enable the tree to establish without competing with weeds for water and food. A mulch of organic matter, such as leaf mould or composted bark, will help retain soil moisture and suppress weeds within the circle. Apply the mulch when the soil is damp, and make sure the mulching material is not in direct contact with the trunk of the tree above the correct soil level.

Don't forget

When you order or buy your trees, buy stakes and ties at the same time so that you have everything ready when you come to plant. If deer or rabbits are a problem, invest in a plastic spiral guard to protect the young bark from damage (see page 59).

HOW TO plant a container-grown tree in a lawn

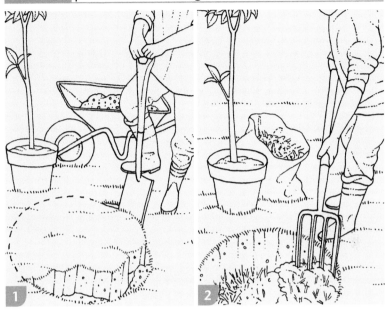

1 Make the planting hole wide enough to allow room for growth – three to four times the width of the pot or rootball – and slightly deeper than the roots.

2 Break up the soil really well with a fork, mixing in a bucket of compost or leaf mould to help it retain moisture. Water the tree before planting.

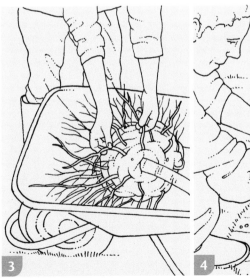

3 Gently tease out any tightly packed roots. Place the tree in the hole, backfill with soil, firming it gently, and water. *See also* Preparation and planting, page 45.

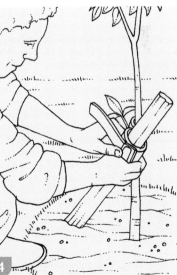

4 A diagonal stake driven into the ground after the tree is planted avoids damage to the rootball. Secure the tree with a purpose-made adjustable tie.

Moving a tree

Moving established trees is a risky business with no guarantee of success. Of course, ideally all trees would be chosen and positioned with much careful forethought, and would not end up in the wrong place. But life isn't like that. Mistakes are made, things change, houses are extended and gardens replanned, and sometimes a tree has to be relocated. If it was planted fairly recently, and is not too large, it may be possible to move the tree successfully.

This flowering crab apple tree may look delightful now, but it's much too close to the house and will soon outgrow its space.

When to move a tree

Winter is normally the best time to move a deciduous tree – while it is dormant. It will then have time to settle before meeting the demands of a new growing season. In the case of an evergreen tree, it may be better to wait until early spring: it can then begin to grow away soon after the move as the soil begins to warm up.

If you are able to plan ahead, especially with larger trees, it is worth cutting a circle with a spade, all the way round the tree, a little way inside the circumference of its leaf canopy. Ideally, you would do this a whole year ahead of the actual move. Cutting through some of the surface roots in this way encourages the tree to make a network of new fibrous roots closer to the trunk, which can help sustain it after a move.

How to move a tree

The perfect tree move is carried out without the tree noticing at all. This is a tall order, but what's critical is to minimize any stress to the tree. Trees largely feed and take up water through fine roots near the surface, so aim to leave these undisturbed in a good rootball with plenty of soil attached.

To prevent delay once the tree has been lifted, prepare the new hole first (see pages 45–6). Make it about 30cm (12in) wider than the expected rootball, and at least as deep. Loosely tie the branches so they don't get in the way. Now lift the tree. This will be easier with a second pair of hands and a tarpaulin (see opposite). Lower the tree into the new hole, checking the depth carefully to ensure that the soil level is the same as it was in the old position. Fill the hole with soil, firming as you go, and water just as for a new tree (see page 47). You will need to provide sturdy support for the tree (see pages 45–6).

Choosing the right season to move a tree may make all the difference.
① Young evergreens such as this yew are best moved in early spring.
② Winter is best for deciduous trees like hornbeam.

Don't forget

It is often worth considering reducing the crown of a tree that is to be moved. This means that the newly transplanted tree can concentrate on re-establishing its roots without also having to sustain a large canopy, which can sometimes result in branches dying back. (See Crown pruning, page 51.)

Follow-up care should include watering in dry spells through the first season – but do avoid creating a swamp. A mulch over the root area will help to preserve moisture. If the tree begins to wilt, try pruning it or at least snip off some of its leaves so that the roots don't have to work so hard.

Using heavy machinery

If a tree or shrub has to be moved because of a building project where there is heavy machinery on site, the services of a skilful and cooperative digger driver can make light work of a job that could otherwise be at best strenuous and at worst impossible. Using machinery may seem brutal, but it is worth a try – even with a sizeable tree, especially if the alternative is to scrap it. The first step is to choose the new location and dig the hole. Then the tree can be lifted with the digger bucket. With care and luck, it will come out of the ground complete with a much larger soil ball around its roots than you could manage by hand. The rootball can then be eased straight into the new hole, settled and watered in.

Will it live?

It's impossible to predict whether a tree move will be successful – there are so many variables: timing, weather, the species of tree, how old or well established it is. Trees with fibrous root systems, like yew, are often good survivors, especially if you leave plenty of soil clinging to the roots. Fast-growing trees like eucalyptus, laburnum and Mount Etna broom (*Genista aetnensis*) tend to be less forgiving – but if you have to start again with a young tree, it will soon match its predecessor. Some trees, such as arbutus and the Mediterranean cypress (*Cupressus sempervirens*), do not transplant well when large, so are best planted as small specimens and left alone.

Don't forget

If you already have a young tree that you suspect may be too close to a building or road, have it inspected by a professional arborist so that you are aware of any potential problems and can move or remove it before it becomes an expensive liability.

HOW TO move a tree

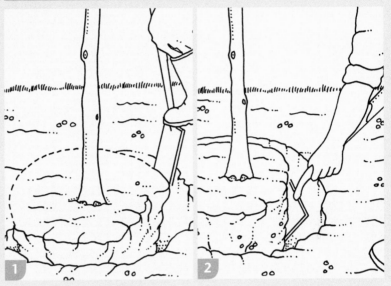

1 Cut a circle all the way round the tree (if you can do this a year in advance, all the better). The circle should be as large as possible – though not so large that you can't move the resulting rootball.

2 Gently use the spade to cut underneath the rootball until you have worked it free all the way round. You will be less likely to cause stress to the tree's roots if you take this stage slowly.

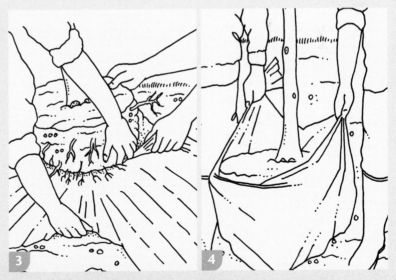

3 Slide a strong tarpaulin or polythene sheet under the rootball. You really need two people at this stage: one to lift the tree and the other to slide the sheet underneath it.

4 Gather up the corners and lift the supported rootball out of the hole. Carry or wheelbarrow the tree to its new home. Don't lift the tree by its trunk. For instructions on replanting, *see* page 47.

Pruning trees

In most cases, pruning a plant is a way of controlling its growth for a particular purpose: usually to influence its shape or size, to prevent congested growth, or to stimulate it into producing more flowers or better foliage. Most trees do not need the kind of routine pruning that is normal for many garden shrubs. Basic tree pruning will typically involve a little formative work to help a young tree develop a good branch framework, and occasional pruning of older specimens to reduce their size or to cut out branches that are badly positioned, damaged or diseased.

When removing a branch, place the saw so it will neither cut into the trunk nor leave a stub that will die back.

Shaping young trees

In the first couple of years after planting, it's a good idea to set your tree on the right track by helping it to develop a balanced, well-shaped head and a clear trunk of the required height – you will probably be continuing a process already started by the tree nursery. Keeping up the good work as the tree grows will help it to age gracefully and should prevent the need for more difficult remedial pruning later.

Creating a standard tree in this way is especially important in a small garden, because trees with a bare trunk and an overhead branch framework have clear space under the canopy that can be used for planting and, eventually, could make a pleasant place for a bench in dappled shade.

Don't let sideshoots compete with the tree's leading shoot, or the tree may become forked and could eventually split. Cut back any shoots that are damaged or crossing. Remove branches that are too low to be part of the crown of the tree, but do this in stages, over several years, first reducing the length of

HOW TO create a standard tree

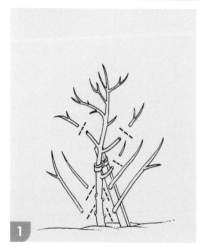

1

At the end of the tree's first winter, cut off the lowest sideshoots close to the main stem and shorten the sideshoots a little higher up the tree.

2

In the second winter, cut off the sideshoots that you had previously shortened; the tree is now beginning to develop a clear trunk.

3

As spring begins, shorten the next tier of branches. Also, cut out crossing branches and any shoots at the top that could overtake the leading shoot.

Crown pruning

Skilful pruning can be invaluable, especially in a small garden. You can reduce, lift or thin the crown of a tree to suit the available space.

CROWN REDUCTION

CROWN LIFTING

CROWN THINNING

each branch and then removing it the following winter. This helps the trunk to develop and strengthen. Aim to gradually create a framework of side branches that are evenly spaced around the trunk.

Pruning: some golden rules

- Use only clean, sharp tools.
- Don't leave 'snags'; cut just above a bud or shoot.
- Remove dead, diseased or crossing branches first.
- When removing a branch, cut just outside the 'collar' or bark ridge where the branch joins the trunk; never cut completely flush with the trunk.
- Don't use wound paint; allow the tree to heal naturally.
- Make an initial cut on the underside of the branch when removing heavy branches, to prevent tearing.

Don't forget

Prune large-leaved evergreens such as laurels and sweet bay with secateurs rather than clipping them with shears, which can cause unsightly brown edges to the cut leaves.

Pruning for maintenance

Have a careful look at your growing trees from time to time to see if any minor surgery is necessary. Any suckers from the rootstock should be removed promptly, as should shoots sprouting from the trunk. If the crown of the tree is becoming congested with thin, whippy shoots or crossing branches, remove these too, along with any diseased or damaged branches.

Pruning mature trees

A healthy tree can easily become too large or too dense for its space, but that need not mean it has to go. The crown, or canopy, of the tree can be thinned, to admit more light; or raised, to give more space underneath; or reduced, to make a smaller and less bulky tree. (*See* Crown pruning, above). A qualified tree surgeon should be able to carry out any of these procedures, and with large trees this is likely to be

the best course of action. On smaller trees you may prefer to tackle the work yourself, but make sure you have good, safe equipment and tools, and protective clothing such as gloves, long sleeves and trousers, and eye protection if necessary.

Pollarding and coppicing

These two rather drastic pruning techniques can be an excellent way of adapting certain trees to small spaces. Coppicing entails cutting a tree down almost to the ground and allowing it to regrow with several stems. It is a traditional way of managing hazel, sweet chestnut and other trees to produce a limitless

What not to prune

While some trees such as box and yew thrive on pruning, others are best left alone unless it is essential to treat damaged branches or to reduce their size. Pruning a birch, for example, can easily spoil its naturally graceful shape, and the same applies to certain conifers.

Long-handled loppers not only reduce the amount of time you have to spend up a ladder; they can also reach awkward places more easily.

Reversion

Variegated trees usually originate as cuttings taken from a naturally occurring mutation in part of a non-variegated plant. It is not uncommon for a variegated plant to produce a shoot with plain green leaves – that is, one that has mutated back again – though some are more likely to do this than others. The variegated Norway maple *Acer platanoides* 'Drummondii' and the variegated *Acer negundo* 'Flamingo' are both rather prone to reversion. Prune out any such shoots without delay, because the plain green leaves photosynthesize more efficiently and the shoots grow more strongly than the variegated ones, and will soon begin to take over. Cut right back into wood that is producing variegated foliage, because if any of the mutated genetic material remains, the reversion will recur.

Preventing bleeding

Trees sometimes 'bleed' or lose sap from cut branches after they are pruned, but any bleeding should be minimal if you prune at the appropriate time. For most deciduous trees this is while they are dormant – never when the sap is rising in spring. Certain trees are especially prone to bleeding, and any pruning should be done in late autumn: these include Japanese maples, birches, walnuts, figs, hornbeams, laburnums and mulberries. You don't need to apply any products or wrapping; the tree will heal itself.

supply of poles without harming the trees, which can be cut every five to seven years. Among the garden trees that lend themselves to this treatment are *Catalpa* (Indian bean tree), *Paulownia* and eucalyptus. Pollarding is a similar procedure but with a tree on a leg or trunk. New growth is cut back each year to its point of origin at the head of the trunk, or sometimes to a basic branch framework. Plane and lime trees in towns and cities are often pollarded every year. *Acer negundo* is an example of a small garden tree that suits this treatment.

When to prune

Most deciduous trees are best pruned when they are dormant in late autumn and through the winter months, though minor pruning to remove suckers and broken twigs can be done at any time. However, cherries and plums (*Prunus*) should be pruned not in winter but when they are in growth, because they are then less likely to contract silver leaf disease (*see* page 59). Late summer is a good time. Evergreen trees are usually best pruned in early spring, just before the soil warms up and encourages them to start growing, or in late summer.

Don't forget

When you are pruning a tree, thinking and looking are at least as important as making the actual cuts. Work out where new growth is likely to be made as a result of each cut, and take time to assess the effect of each before you make it. If in doubt, delay cutting until you're sure. Once those loppers have snapped shut, there's no going back!

Growing shrubs as trees

Broadly speaking, most of us can tell a tree from a shrub, yet the distinction is not always clear-cut. It's mostly to do with size, number of main stems and bushiness. But many familiar shrubs can be pruned to make them more like trees, with one or more bare stems supporting a crown held well clear of the ground. Roses, fuchsias and bay are popular as standards, but there's a whole range of other shrubs that can be pruned into tree-like plants, extending the options for small gardens.

Creating space

You might think a tree would take up more space than a shrub, but that's not necessarily so. A deciduous tree with a clear stem has valuable growing space underneath it that you don't find beneath a dense, bushy shrub. On the other hand, if you prune a shrub to give it a clear stem, you can use the space beneath its branches. The shade cast by the shrub's summer leaf canopy, and plenty of light in winter and spring before the leaves appear, provide ideal conditions for a range of woodland plants such as spring bulbs and ground-covering perennials. Include some plants with interesting foliage to create a tapestry effect that will last all summer.

Shaping shrubs to make small trees will give many more planting possibilities. Among those that work well are:

① *Sambucus nigra* 'Eva'.

② *Callicarpa bodinieri* var. *giraldii* 'Profusion'.

③ *Cotinus coggygria* Purpureus Group.

Evergreen shrubs as trees

Sometimes you may need a plant to provide year-round screening or structure, or a permanent focal point, without gobbling up valuable ground space. Formal 'lollipops' of box, holly or bay are popular, but there are other options. Try *Photinia* × *fraseri*, with its bright red young foliage, and a *Viburnum tinus* or a camellia, both so welcome for late-winter or early-spring flowers. Cultivars of *Elaeagnus* × *ebbingei* or of *Euonymus japonicus* are possibilities if you want a variegated plant. These can all be bought as ready-trained standards (though they tend to be expensive), or you can shape a young plant yourself by removing sideshoots (*see* right). Plants trained and used in this way become even more versatile when grown in large pots that can be moved around when you fancy a change.

The practicalities

The best shrubs to transform into tree-like plants are those that produce long, straightish stems. Avoid anything bushy, or with a weeping habit, as well as shrubs that make a lot of vigorous new shoots from the base such as *Cornus alba* (dogwood) cultivars.

Begin with a newly rooted cutting or a young plant and remove sideshoots from the base of the main stem or stems. Work upwards gradually as the plant grows, until you have bare stems of the required length, with the crown of the plant beginning at the height you had in mind. As the plant matures, remove any low sideshoots as soon as you see them developing.

More good shrubs to grow as trees

Buddleja alternifolia
Clerodendrum trichotomum var. *fargesii*
Elaeagnus 'Quicksilver'
Euonymus europaeus 'Red Cascade'
Hamamelis
Hibiscus syriacus
Olearia macrodonta
Syringa

Propagating trees

There is something magical about creating your own plants from scratch, and trees – owing to their size and longevity – can be especially rewarding to propagate. It is rather pleasing to imagine future generations sitting under a tree that you have grown from a seed or cutting. Propagating trees is a fun project for plant enthusiasts, and a great experiment to try if you garden with children.

Growing trees from seed

Many trees, especially native species, are easy to grow from seed. Of course, if you are very successful, you may not have space for the resulting forest, but friends with larger gardens may welcome your surplus young trees, or perhaps you could donate them to a local community or school tree-planting scheme. The Tree Council's website (www.treecouncil. org.uk) has information on growing trees from seed and on getting involved in local planting schemes.

In autumn and early winter, gather a selection of nuts and other tree seeds. Types likely to be successful are hazelnuts, walnuts, acorns and horse chestnuts. Ripe berries such as those of native hawthorn, holly and rowan, are also fun to try, but these are designed to germinate after passing through the gut of a bird, and are more likely to succeed if you separate the seeds from the flesh of the berries (by soaking the berries in water) before sowing. Sow nuts and seeds in deep pots, with each

Don't forget

The seeds of several trees found in gardens, such as laburnum and yew, are poisonous. Be very alert and careful, especially if you are gardening with children.

Once it has a few leaves, transfer your infant tree into a larger pot to give its roots more room to develop.

Some seeds to sow for fun

Gather hazelnuts in autumn; shake the seeds from ripe female birch catkins from late summer on; pick hawthorn berries in autumn and holly berries in winter. Sow nuts and seeds in pots and leave them outside to germinate over winter.

| HAZELNUTS | FEMALE BIRCH CATKINS | HAWTHORN BERRIES | HOLLY BERRIES |

covered by roughly its own depth of compost. Label the pots and leave them outdoors in a sheltered place. Alternatively, sow the seeds in the open ground – in a place where you won't forget them. Cover them with netting to prevent mice and squirrels from digging them up – they are especially fond of nuts! The seeds of most trees will need to spend a winter outdoors before they will germinate, so be patient. Don't let the pots become waterlogged, and don't let them dry out either.

Growing trees from cuttings

Many trees can be propagated from cuttings of various types, but hardwood cuttings are the easiest. Take them in winter, when the plant is dormant, and root them outdoors. The easiest tree cuttings, such as willows and elders, may even begin to grow roots in a jar of water. You

Grafting

Many garden trees that you buy will have been grafted and are generally easy to recognize because they have a bulge or ridge on the trunk, usually just above ground level. This is the 'graft union', where the graft was made when the tree was in its infancy. A cutting or bud (known as the scion) of a particular variety of apple or flowering cherry, for example, would have been expertly grafted onto a rootstock of a different one. In the case of fruit such as apples, pears and plums, specially raised rootstocks are chosen that limit the size of the resulting tree while enabling it to flower and bear fruit at an earlier age.

Don't forget

Since the rootstock of a grafted ornamental tree will usually be a less desirable wild form and may be more vigorous than your chosen tree, any suckers from the stock must be removed to prevent it taking over.

HOW TO take hardwood cuttings

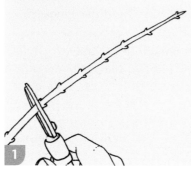

1. Remove a firm, ripe shoot no more than a year old, cutting just above a leaf joint (to stop die-back on the parent plant). Re-trim the lower end below a leaf joint, as shown.

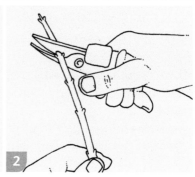

2. Trim the cutting at the top, just above another leaf-joint. Take off any sideshoots. The trimmed cuttings should be 15–30cm (6–12in) long.

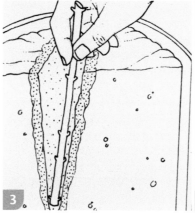

3. Keeping the cuttings the right way up, push them to about two-thirds of their depth into a pot of gritty, free-draining compost or into a slit trench in the garden. Label them so you know what they are.

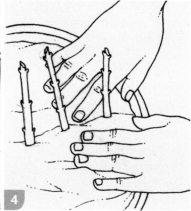

4. Firm the soil around the cuttings, leaving no air pockets. Water to settle them, then leave them to root over the winter. Don't let them dry out. When they show strong new growth, pot them up individually.

are unlikely to want the wild forms of either in your garden, of course, but try one of the ornamental elders with purple or variegated leaves, or the twisted willow (*Salix babylonica* var. *pekinensis* 'Tortuosa'), a novelty plant that can be grown in a container when small, and kept going by taking cuttings every few years. Sometimes called the

dragon's-claw willow, it has twisty, golden stems that make a particularly eye-catching feature when they are leafless in winter.

Don't forget

Remember that propagating a tree from seed will not result in a genetically identical plant, so cultivated varieties will not come true. These must be propagated from cuttings.

Tree problems and remedies

There may be more garden pests and diseases now than ever before, but it is best to cultivate a relaxed attitude towards most of them and try not to get downhearted. Good gardening is a better (and far more enjoyable) way to keep problems at bay than a shed full of potions – so grow your trees well, vary your plantings, practise good garden hygiene and encourage natural predators. Lots of information and photographs can be found on the Internet to help identify pests and diseases and recognize the really serious ones. If you decide on spraying as a last resort, check online for up-to-date legislation and recommendations.

Common pests

Aphids

Greenfly, blackfly and woolly aphids are some of the many types of aphid that affect trees. These suck the sap and excrete sticky honeydew, which attracts sooty moulds onto the leaves. Most aphids are specific to certain host plants: cherry blackfly, for example, often infest young shoots of cherry trees.

Prevention and control
Encouraging birds such as wrens and blue tits, as well as insect predators such as hoverflies and ladybirds whose larvae eat aphids, will reduce numbers dramatically. In localized infestations the aphids can be washed or rubbed off affected leaves.

Bark beetles

Many beetle species tunnel into wood to lay their eggs – from the domestic furniture beetle that causes 'woodworm' to the beetles that carry the devastating Dutch elm disease. Different beetle species attack different trees; for example, the shot-hole borer tends to go for fruit trees. Signs of their presence are small holes where the larvae have emerged after hatching, and/or 'galleries' of tunnels just beneath the bark.

Prevention and control Keep trees healthy by maintaining good growing conditions, and by pruning out dead or damaged wood. Beetles are more likely to choose wood that is dead or dying, and their presence may indicate that the tree already has a problem such as fungal infection. Certain birds, especially great spotted woodpeckers, find beetle larvae delicious and are well equipped to extract them.

Bay sucker

Curled leaf margins on a bay tree are usually a sign of this aphid-like insect, which sucks sap from young leaves of sweet bay (*Laurus nobilis*). Inside the rolled-under leaf edges you may find tiny, greyish nymphs nestling in a whitish waxy substance. Affected leaf tissue usually turns yellow before developing brown, dry patches. A bad infestation can make a bay tree look very unsightly.

Prevention and control Pick off and destroy affected leaves on smaller specimens, and try spraying inside the bush with a jet from a hose, which will dislodge some of the insects. Keep bushes well watered and growing strongly, to help them resist attack.

Caterpillars

These larvae of butterflies, moths and sawflies all devour plant material. Their activities are usually most obvious in the form of holes in leaves and many different trees can be affected. Young plants or whole branches can be stripped bare if severe infestations occur: spindle trees (*Euonymus*), for example, may suffer attacks by ermine moths, which cover the trees with silken webbing.

Prevention and control Caterpillars are a nutritious food for the young of many birds, so encourage these natural predators into your garden to control populations. Picking off the caterpillars by hand is also fairly effective.

Codling moth

This small moth lays its eggs on tiny developing apples. When the eggs hatch, the caterpillars tunnel inside the apple to feed, and the fruit can subsequently rot.

Prevention and control Buy special pheromone traps that lure the male moths inside, preventing them from mating with the females.

Leaf miners

Holly and horse chestnut are just two of the trees that can be affected by leaf miners, the larvae of various insects that feed inside leaves, making visible tunnels within the leaf tissue.

Prevention and control Small localized attacks (for example on holly) can be contained by removing affected leaves, but where the whole tree is infested – as often happens with horse chestnut – there is little you can do. Spraying with pesticides tends to be ineffective because the larvae are protected by the leaf's outer surfaces.

Scale insects

Trees with leathery leaves, such as bay and citrus, tend to suffer from these pests, especially when they are grown in pots.

Scale insects don't really look like insects at all: they're just flat specks, in different shades of brown, stuck individually like miniscule limpets to stems and the undersides of leaves. Like aphids, they suck sap and excrete honeydew, which then attracts unsightly moulds.

Prevention and control Scale insects can be rubbed off with your fingers or with a cloth or cotton bud dampened with a detergent solution. Infestations seldom reach plague proportions. The best thing is to be aware of the problem and remove the insects whenever you see them.

Common diseases

Apple and pear scab

Pears, apples and crab apples all quite commonly suffer from scab disease, which causes rough, brown corky patches on the skin of the fruit. The inside of the fruit may be unaffected in some cases and can be eaten if carefully peeled. In other cases, a bad attack of scab can prevent the fruit from developing. Sometimes the affected areas of the fruit surface will crack and allow rots and other diseases to attack the fruit.

Prevention and control Don't allow branches to become overcrowded. Good pruning is the best preventative measure, improving air circulation so that the still, damp conditions that encourage fungal spores do not develop. Some varieties are resistant, such as the well-known 'Discovery' apple. After a bad attack, clear away fallen leaves in autumn to help prevent spores from overwintering and reinfecting the tree.

Box blight

Box (*Buxus sempervirens*), especially when used in formal hedging and topiary, is often disfigured by one of two increasingly widespread fungal diseases that cause the stems and leaves to die off in patches. The more serious is *Cylindrocladium buxicola*, typified by brown or black spots on the leaves and sometimes white webbing on the undersides. *Volutella*, the other one, causes leaves to turn brown and develop a pinkish mould underneath.

Prevention and control Trim box when the weather is dry, and clean tools thoroughly afterwards to prevent cross-infection. Cut out and carefully dispose of infected branches. The cultivar *Buxus microphylla* 'Faulkner' is said to have some resistance. If the problem is persistent, grow a different evergreen instead: the small-leaved holly *Ilex crenata* 'Convexa' looks very similar to box.

Bracket fungus

Any fungal bracket growing on the trunk of an old tree is a bad sign, indicating that the tree is infected with some kind of heart rot or fungal disease that will probably kill all or part of it eventually. Large trees that develop brackets should be inspected by a tree surgeon and felled if they are considered dangerous: diseased trees can shed limbs without warning and are especially vulnerable in high winds. **Prevention and control** Trees can pick up fungal infections in many ways: through pruning cuts or damaged bark, for example, or if the soil becomes waterlogged. There may be little you can do except prune carefully and correctly, with clean tools.

Cankers

If you spot lesions in the bark of a tree, especially if they are oozing sap, you should suspect canker. Most likely to occur in fruit trees and rowans, it is caused by one of several types of bacterial or fungal infection.

Prevention and control Keep a close watch on trees and cut out any affected branches before the disease spreads and kills the tree. There is no cure, but well-grown trees will be less susceptible.

Coral spot

Acer and *Elaeagnus* are particularly susceptible to this distinctive and common fungal disease that can

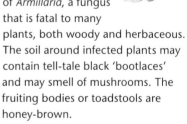

cause branches to wilt and die quite suddenly. It may be some time before small, pinkish-orange pustules appear from the dead wood, identifying the cause. The fungus also attacks many other species as well, and can continue to grow on dead wood.

Prevention and control Prune out affected branches until you reach healthy wood. Burn or dispose of infected prunings. Always use sharp, clean secateurs when carrying out routine pruning, taking care not to leave snags through which the spores could enter more easily.

Fireblight

This is an unpleasant and serious bacterial disease that can affect many fruit- and berry-bearing plants such as apples, pears, rowans and hawthorns (though not cherries and plums). Cotoneaster and pyracantha are also susceptible. Plants pick up fireblight through the flowers, and these die off and hang down. The same thing happens to the leaves and the plant looks scorched. Infected wood may be reddish-brown beneath the bark.

Prevention and control It may be possible to save plants that are only partially affected by cutting out affected branches, pruning well into

Don't forget

All trees will be healthier and more able to shrug off diseases and pests without serious damage if they have the right growing conditions. Most are not too fussy, but choose varieties carefully for challenging conditions such as damp gardens or thin, shallow, chalky soil (see pages 60–7). Make sure your trees also have the food and water they need.

healthy wood. Badly affected plants should be destroyed. If fireblight has been a problem, avoid growing trees known to be susceptible, such as *Sorbus* 'Joseph Rock' and *Sorbus vilmorinii*. Certain cultivars, on the other hand, are known to have some resistance, such as the crab apple *Malus* 'Evereste'.

Honey fungus

This is probably the disease that gardeners dread the most. The name covers several species of *Armillaria*, a fungus that is fatal to many plants, both woody and herbaceous. The soil around infected plants may contain tell-tale black 'bootlaces' and may smell of mushrooms. The fruiting bodies or toadstools are honey-brown.

Prevention and control There are no effective controls, but certain trees, including *Acer negundo*, bay, box, hornbeam and yew, have some resistance. Birches, apples, cherries and lilacs are among those that are particularly susceptible. Remove affected plants as quickly and as thoroughly as you can. It may be possible to stop the fungus spreading to healthy plants by sinking barriers of heavy-gauge polythene into the ground, but this is by no means foolproof.

Peach leaf curl

Ornamental cherries sometimes contract this disfiguring fungal disease, though it is much more common in peaches, apricots and almonds. It is identified by reddish blistering on young leaves, which take on a dusty-white appearance before dying and falling off.

Prevention and control Remove affected leaves and wait for new growth, helping this along with feeding and watering if necessary. Spraying in autumn with a copper-based fungicide such as Bordeaux mixture will give some protection. If the problem persists, replace with other species.

Powdery mildew

Apple and crab apple trees are among many plants that suffer from a range of different powdery mildews. The disease shows as a whitish bloom on the leaves, which may become misshapen and eventually shrivel and die. Young shoots suffer most.

Prevention and control Good air circulation around trees and keeping roots moist are the best preventative measures. Avoid buying trees that are particularly susceptible, such as purple-leaved crab apples, or buy resistant varieties (in the case of purple-leaved crab apples, *Malus* 'Directeur Moerlands' is one such).

Don't forget

Ornamental crab apples (*Malus*) take more kindly to pruning than flowering cherries and plums (*Prunus*), which are inclined to pick up diseases through pruning cuts. This may be an important consideration if your tree will need to be pruned regularly, to keep it to size.

Silver leaf disease

Cherries and plums are susceptible to this fungal disease, which gives the leaves on affected branches a silvery sheen on their upper surface. Cut stems will be brown inside, and without intervention the fungus may kill the tree.

Prevention and control Silver leaf disease is much more likely to occur if cherries and plums are pruned when dormant, so do your pruning when the tree is in growth: that way, the cuts will heal more readily. Late summer is a good time. If the disease strikes, prune out any affected branches without delay, cutting back some 15cm (6in) into healthy wood.

Sudden oak death

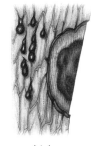

This alarming disease, introduced into Britain relatively recently, is caused by a swiftly acting fungus called *Phytophthora ramorum*, which can be lethal to certain trees and shrubs – for example beeches, rhododendrons and viburnums, among others. It enters the tree from the base of the trunk, and may manifest itself through cankers, often low down on the trunk, that drip brown or black liquid. There may be a red or brown rot beneath the bark, and leaves may carry brown marks.

Prevention and control This is a notifiable disease that must be reported to your local authority. It is difficult to diagnose and needs expert identification. Affected trees have to be destroyed to prevent the infection from spreading.

Dealing with pests and diseases

Many garden chemicals once used to treat serious problems such as honey fungus have been withdrawn from sale, so the only current option with such fatal diseases is to remove and destroy the affected tree. Think twice before reaching for the spray gun to treat less serious problems, because the tree will often recover by itself, particularly if the affected shoots or leaves are removed promptly, or if predators move in to devour the pests. In the case of persistent trouble with host-specific ailments, such as box blight, bay sucker and holly leaf blight, the best solution is to replace the affected plants with something different.

Four-legged pests

Deer, rabbits and squirrels can all be very bad news for garden trees, especially for young specimens: these do not have the reserves to withstand much damage to their bark or shoots. Tree guards are essential to protect young saplings where any of these animals is a problem. The simplest guards, usually made of plastic in a spiral or tubular shape, will give limited protection, but you may need to build something taller and more robust, such as a secure enclosure of wire mesh or stout metal fencing, especially if the problem is deer.

Don't forget

Disinfect saws and secateurs that have been used to prune diseased plants. Don't compost diseased prunings or leave them lying around; burn them or dispose of them through a municipal garden waste scheme, where they will be composted at high temperatures.

Trees for challenging sites

Most garden trees, once they are established, will thrive in a reasonably wide range of soils and conditions. However difficult your soil or awkward the site, your chosen tree will have the best chance of flourishing if it is one that has a natural preference for your particular growing conditions. You will have noticed that wild trees often grow in the most inhospitable places, and the right tree for even the most disobliging garden will be out there somewhere. If you choose well, your tree could be with you for a long time, so it's worth a little trouble to consider what it should be.

Tiny spaces

It's easy to assume that a tiny garden has no space for a tree, but it's worth finding room for one if you possibly can. Making the most of a small space involves using all three dimensions. A carefully chosen, compact tree is an ideal way to bring height into the picture, as well as providing screening, a focal point and a calming mass of greenery that will be life-enhancing for both you and your garden wildlife.

Something special

Owners of small gardens may bemoan the lack of space, but a compact garden has advantages that larger plots may lack. In a small town garden or sheltered courtyard you can experiment with choice plants, including trees, that would not be happy in cold, exposed gardens. *Albizia julibrissin* f. *rosea* is one example – a delightful and unusual little tree that needs a sheltered spot; others are *Acacia baileyana* 'Purpurea', *Robinia* × *slavinii* 'Hillieri' and *Cercis canadensis* 'Forest Pansy'. A handsome and unusual aromatic evergreen for a mild, sheltered garden is the South American *Drimys winteri*, with scented, white flowers in late spring.

Small spaces are very good for making the most of fragrant trees,

Lilac, pruned to form a small tree, makes a good screen and will fill a front garden with fragrance in spring. A clematis could be added for later interest.

trapping scent that might otherwise be whisked away on the wind. *Azara microphylla*, *Osmanthus* × *burkwoodii*, lilac, hawthorn and certain flowering cherries are all strongly fragrant. A compact garden also enables you to appreciate the more subtle scents that might easily go unnoticed in a larger area. Apple and rowan blossom do not produce the boldest of plant perfumes, but in a confined space on a warm day you'll savour every whiff.

Slender trees

Narrow, vertical evergreens are well worth considering for a small space. Carefully positioned, they contribute valuable structure as well as screening to break up or blot out unwanted views. If you can use two or three, they will add an element of harmony and rhythm to the garden plan. Irish yew (*Taxus baccata* 'Fastigiata') is a winner, and can be

clipped to keep it as narrow as you like. Other slender evergreens you might consider include *Juniperus communis* 'Hibernica' and *Ilex aquifolium* 'Green Pillar'.

Tiny-space pruning tactics

The range of trees you can grow in a very small garden increases if you don't mind a fairly radical pruning session once a year. Pollarding is a useful technique for adapting certain trees to small spaces, and crown lifting makes more usable space beneath a tree. Compact trees can often be created from plants often usually thought of as shrubs. (*See* pages 51–3 for pruning techniques.)

Don't forget

You can double the impact of a tree by using it to support a climber with a different season of interest. A summer-flowering clematis, for example, will bridge the gap between spring blossom and autumn berries. Make sure it has its fair share of food and water, though.

More trees for tiny spaces

Acer palmatum 'Sango-kaku' (*see* page 70)

Cotoneaster 'Hybridus Pendulus' (*see* page 76)

Juniperus communis 'Hibernica'

Laurus nobilis (*see* page 80)

Malus × *robusta* 'Red Sentinel' (*see* page 82)

Osmanthus × *burkwoodii* (*see* page 84)

Sorbus vilmorinii (*see* page 91)

Taxus baccata 'Standishii' – slow-growing, slim, columnar yew; golden foliage

Shady gardens

A good tactic for shady gardens is to choose and locate your trees and other plants to make the most of the available light. A garden shaded by buildings, for example, might be sunny for part of the day when the sun reaches it, or in summer when the sun is high in the sky. If the shade is cast by large deciduous trees, more light will be available in winter and early spring, when the branches are bare.

Natural shade-lovers

In the wild, some trees grow very happily in places where they are shaded by the canopy of other, larger trees. Many of them are evergreens: their leaves can mop up light until their deciduous neighbours come to life in spring and shelter them from the hot summer sun. Holly, box and yew all grow like this in temperate woodlands and are good trees for shady gardens: all can be pruned repeatedly or clipped into formal shapes. This makes them doubly valuable where space is restricted. Native deciduous trees that are reasonably shade-tolerant include hazel and hawthorn.

A surprising number of exotic trees, which dislike exposure to hot, drying sun and cold winds, are also happier in some shade, protected by other trees around them. Examples include many of the Japanese maples (*Acer palmatum*), *Nyssa sinensis* and *Stewartia pseudocamellia*.

Low autumn sunshine highlights the elegant, spreading canopy of a skilfully positioned Japanese maple.

Golden foliage

Golden leaves make a good substitute for sunshine in a dim space. A north-facing garden will be considerably brightened by a golden *Catalpa* or *Gleditsia*, or perhaps *Ulmus × hollandica* 'Dampieri Aurea', a conical, golden-leaved hybrid elm resistant to Dutch elm disease. As an alternative to a fully fledged tree, consider a golden-leaved Japanese maple, or an ornamental elder, *Sambucus nigra* 'Aurea' or *Sambucus racemosa* 'Sutherland Gold'. Note, though, that for the best colouring most golden-leaved plants need a certain amount of light, so don't plant these in the deepest shade.

Variegated trees

A semi-shady setting makes the best kind of backdrop for trees and shrubs that have interesting leaf variegations, showing up their beautiful patterning while also preventing the more delicate white areas of the leaves from scorching. The two popular variegated dogwoods *Cornus controversa* 'Variegata' and *Cornus alternifolia* 'Argentea' look their most elegant out of strong sunlight, and the same applies to the white-variegated shrubs – for example some cultivars of *Pittosporum tenuifolium* – that can take on the role of trees in small gardens. White flowers, silvery leaves and pale bark (like that of birch) all show up better against a dark background such as a brick wall or tall evergreen hedge that may shade them for part of the day.

More trees for shady gardens

Aucuba japonica 'Marmorata' – tough, variegated evergreen shrub that can be pruned to form a small tree

Cotoneaster frigidus 'Cornubia' (*see* page 76)

Ilex × altaclerensis 'Golden King' (*see* page 79)

Photinia × fraseri 'Red Robin' (*see* page 85)

Prunus lusitanica (*see* page 25)

Sorbus cashmiriana (*see* page 91)

Windy gardens

Many trees depend on wind for pollination, and breezy conditions also help keep trees cool, discouraging certain pests and diseases such as fungal infections. On the other hand, wind-scorched young foliage is a sorry sight, as is the more dramatic damage that gales inflict, breaking off branches and sometimes smashing whole trees. Trees adapted to windy conditions will typically have leaves that are either leathery and tough (to resist the force of the wind), or small and narrow (to allow it to pass through without too much resistance).

Resilient natives

British gardens have to contend with a range of breezy conditions from mild, damp Atlantic westerlies to chilly east winds from mainland Europe, so it is not surprising that many of our native trees are pretty wind-tolerant. Among the toughest are hawthorns, birches, rowans and pines, which are often used in shelter belts. All grow happily in cold, exposed places, and their

With regular pruning and support for its trunk, the native coastal shrub sea buckthorn will make a small, silver-leaved, berrying tree.

many fairly compact cultivars add up to a wide range of trees suitable for windy gardens (*see Betula, Crataegus, Pinus, Sorbus*, pages 68–91). These are generally less risky than the many exotic trees that are native to sheltered mountain valleys or woodlands, where the effects of wild weather are less damaging. Certainly, any trees with large, soft leaves or fragile flowers are best avoided in windy gardens.

Coastal gardens

Gardens near the sea can be the windiest of all, but they seldom suffer from the penetrating cold that can make life hard for trees in the chilliest inland gardens, so you can include some slightly more tender trees in your shortlist. Remember that many plants can be damaged by salt spray, which is sometimes blown a surprisingly long way inland. Among the plants that can withstand salt-laden winds are *Arbutus unedo*, with its leathery leaves, and various fine-leaved plants that filter the wind. These include pines, sea buckthorn (*Hippophae rhamnoides*) and juniper.

Don't forget

In exposed gardens it's vital that you check trees regularly, even if they are well established. Make sure ties and stakes on young trees are secure, and prune out any weak or damaged growth as soon as you see it – rough weather could make it much worse.

More trees for windy gardens

Crataegus crus-galli (*see* page 77)
Elaeagnus angustifolia (*see* page 64)
Pinus sylvestris 'Watereri' – compact, slow-growing cultivar of Scots pine
Salix exigua (*see* page 89)
Sorbus intermedia (*see* page 91)
Tamarix ramosissima – small seaside tree or shrub; feathery foliage, pink flowers

Small beginnings

Establishing trees on windy sites is easier with small specimens. They are more likely to be flexible and will soon adapt to the conditions. With fast-growing trees such as birches and hawthorns, it may be worth considering planting them as young 'whips', like those used for hedging. They will establish quickly and soon catch up with trees planted at a larger size. Be sure to stake new trees (large ones in particular) especially firmly in windy locations (*see* pages 45–6).

Dry gardens

Gardeners with plots on free-draining sand and other light soils have all the luck in winter, when it is seldom too sodden for planting trees, and again in spring, when the soil warms up with enviable speed and all new plants get off to a flying start. Dry summers, on the other hand, are a different matter. New plantings, even of reasonably drought-tolerant species, are especially vulnerable for their first couple of years, and even established trees can struggle when both soil moisture and nutrients are in short supply for an extended period.

A flowering Mount Etna broom brings a memorable touch of the Mediterranean to a dry garden where space is not too tight.

Improving the soil

Free-draining soils that contain a high proportion of sand or gravel have a loose structure and, when they need to, roots can easily penetrate far below the surface to find moisture. You can help light soil hang on to its moisture by digging in organic matter before you plant: well-rotted garden compost, manure or leaf mould all contribute to the process of soil improvement. Keeping the ground beneath the tree's canopy covered – with a mulch of compost or chipped bark, ground-cover planting or gravel, applied when the soil is damp – will reduce evaporation. All these measures will help the roots cope when the crunch comes and there's a prolonged drought; improving the soil in this way will also increase the range of trees you can grow.

A helping hand

The good thing about well-drained soils is that they have the effect of helping slightly tender plants get through the winter, because they prevent waterlogging and they warm up earlier in spring. Many trees and other plants native to Mediterranean areas, such as the Mount Etna broom (*Genista aetnensis*) and the Judas tree (*Cercis siliquastrum*) dislike permanent winter wet and may rot away where cold weather and sodden soil conspire against them. But with dry feet they are much more likely to sail through hard weather. The same applies to the Australian bottlebrush (*Callistemon*) and *Hibiscus syriacus*, a hardy shrub or small tree with lovely trumpet-shaped blooms.

Tree tips for dry gardens

■ Plant trees in autumn so they have the whole winter to establish before they have to cope with possible drought.

■ Mulch a circle of ground around each newly planted tree with compost, chipped bark or leaf mould, applying the mulch when the soil is damp.

■ Water newly planted trees in the evening so that they can take up moisture overnight, when evaporation will be minimal.

■ In drought conditions, cut the bottom off a plastic bottle and sink the bottle upside down into the soil near the base of a newly planted tree. When watering, use the bottle to direct the water straight down to the roots.

More trees for dry gardens

Acer negundo and cultivars (*see* page 71)

Albizia julibrissin f. *rosea* (*see* page 69)

Betula pendula (*see* page 73)

Cotoneaster frigidus 'Cornubia' (*see* page 76)

Elaeagnus angustifolia – scaly branches; narrow leaves, silvery beneath; small, fragrant, yellowish flowers

Gleditsia triacanthos (*see* page 79)

Pinus pinea (*see* page 85)

Sorbus aria 'Lutescens' (*see* page 91)

Damp gardens

It's easy to forget that trees need air, as well as soil and water, around their roots. Soil that is compacted can be a problem, and soil that's waterlogged for long periods can be even worse: as well as preventing air from reaching the roots, it encourages fungal diseases and rots that can be fatal to many trees. But don't despair. There are some trees that love having wet feet, and in the case of many others, some careful ground preparation may enable them to lead a comfortable life in a damp garden.

The unusual small deciduous tree *Nyssa sinensis* is useful for its tolerance of both damp soil and shade. Its real moment of glory comes in the autumn.

Attractive moisture-lovers

In common with certain other moisture-loving plants, many of the most indestructible trees for wet sites – notably willows or poplars – are much too vigorous for small gardens. Their roots can travel a long way rather quickly, in search of water, and it's best to avoid having them anywhere near buildings, hard surfaces or drains. Fortunately, there are much happier solutions.

Amelanchiers, for example, are among the finest of small trees in any garden, looking pretty from the moment the dainty flowers open in spring, and ending the season with glowing autumn colour before leaf fall. They thrive in all but the driest soils, yet are quite tolerant of moist ground, and make a very good choice for a small garden with damp soil. Like amelanchier, *Nyssa sinensis* is often multi-stemmed. Its young leaves turn from bronze to green, then brilliant red in autumn.

Wetland trees

In the wild, alders are among the classic wetland trees but many, including the common alder, *Alnus glutinosa*, grow too large for most gardens. Fortunately, two less vigorous alder cultivars are also very ornamental, and just as good for wildlife: *Alnus glutinosa* 'Imperialis', with fern-like foliage, and golden-leaved *Alnus incana* 'Aurea' (*see* page 69). The miniature cones that grace these trees in winter contain seeds that may well attract flocks of feeding greenfinches and siskins.

A much more compact damp-loving native is the alder buckthorn (*Frangula alnus*, *see* page 19). One of the two British native hawthorns, *Crataegus laevigata*, grows quite happily on sticky clay. Its cultivar 'Crimson Cloud' (*see* page 77) is becoming better known as a small, attractive garden tree. Its deep-pink flowers each have a white eye.

More trees for damp gardens

Betula nigra (*see* page 73)

Carpinus caroliniana – rounded shape; attractive bark; excellent autumn colour

Cryptomeria japonica Elegans Group (*see* page 25)

Mespilus germanica (*see* page 84)

Sorbus aucuparia (*see* page 90)

Tree tips for damp gardens

■ Plant in early spring rather than in autumn or winter, so that trees can grow away without having their roots sitting in water for a long time.

■ Add grit to the soil to assist drainage.

■ Don't dig planting holes until you are ready to plant, especially if the ground is so wet that the holes begin to fill up with water.

■ Keep an eye open for early signs of fungal diseases.

Acid soil

Woodlands with acid soil are widespread in the wild, and plant hunters introduced many of our most desirable garden trees and shrubs from such habitats around the world, mainly in the Far East and North America. Here, woodlands on acid clay or on poor, sandy soils are home to more familiar trees. So gardeners with acid soil have quite an extensive range of trees to choose from.

The fragile, long-stalked, white bells of *Styrax japonicus* are perhaps the daintiest blossom on any tree.

The choicest trees

Good, lime-free soil that is not too dry offers a wonderful opportunity to try some out-of-the-ordinary small trees that are mainly seen in the gardens of connoisseurs and in tree collections. Some have particularly lovely flowers. These range from the white, snowdrop-like blooms of *Halesia monticola* var. *vestita* or the delicate bells of *Styrax japonicus* to the amazing, bright orange-red blossom of the Chilean fire bush, *Embothrium coccineum* – always a conversation piece, but suitable only for mild gardens.

A notable feature of other acid-lovers – for example *Stewartia pseudocamellia* and *Nyssa sinensis* (*see* page 65) – is their flamboyant foliage display in autumn: many trees colour more dramatically on acid soil.

Choice trees like these are worth attempting only if you can offer them optimum conditions. They are woodlanders, appreciating shelter from cold winds and growing best with other plants around them to give protection, humidity and a little shade. As to soil, their preference is for leafy, humus-rich ground that does not dry out. Most of them dislike being disturbed, so they are best planted as small, pot-grown specimens. Nurturing them to flowering size can be tricky and may take some years, but if you succeed with these glorious prima donnas of the garden, it will certainly have been well worth the wait.

Glamorous but a bit temperamental: the unusual Chilean fire bush, *Embothrium coccineum*.

Slightly less choosy customers for acid soil include some of the magnolias (*see* page 81) and flowering dogwoods such as varieties of *Cornus florida*. Most witch hazels (*Hamamelis*) enjoy acid conditions. Though these are often seen as shrubs, they can be shaped into attractive small, spreading trees that hold out their delicate, fragrant late-winter blooms for you at eye (and nose) level – a really special feature at a bleak time of year.

Everyday acid-lovers

Not everyone wants rare treasures to fuss over, and if your acid soil is poor and dry you may in any case have to look elsewhere. The tough native trees birch, holly and rowan all tolerate thin, sandy, acid soil and are undemanding once well established. For something more unusual, try one of the cultivars of *Acer negundo*, known as the box elder, though it has no connection with box or elder. Its other common name, ash-leaved maple, describes it better. 'Flamingo' (*see* page 71) is the best-known form; others to consider are 'Kelly's Gold', the white-variegated 'Variegatum' and 'Elegans', which has yellow-edged leaves.

More trees for acid soil

Acer davidii 'George Forrest' (*see* page 71)
Acer griseum (*see* page 71)
Acer palmatum (*see* page 70)
Cornus kousa var. *chinensis* (*see* page 75)
Eucryphia glutinosa (*see* page 78)
Gleditsia triacanthos 'Sunburst' (*see* page 79)
Hoheria sexstylosa 'Stardust' – upright, glossy-leaved evergreen; pure white, scented flowers in midsummer
Magnolia 'Heaven Scent' (*see* page 81)

Chalky soil

The well-known lime-hating plants such as rhododendrons and camellias are unlikely to succeed on chalk, but in the case of a surprising number of other plants it is the dryness of chalk, rather than its alkalinity, that is the problem. Build a shortlist of your favourite drought-tolerant trees to choose from and also consider improving the soil to help it retain moisture, so you can increase the range of trees that you can grow.

A compact and decorative tree, *Cotoneaster* 'Hybridus Pendulus' is ideal for chalky soil.

Planting in chalky soil

Chalky gardens range from those with hopelessly shallow topsoil overlying solid chalk to those that have a reasonable depth of topsoil over a free-draining base; the latter can be positively advantageous to gardeners and plants, especially in wet winters. In the case of extremely shallow soil, planting any sort of tree is beset with problems, and there's really no alternative to the hard work of breaking up the solid chalk beneath the topsoil before planting if the tree is to have any chance of success. However, it is now known that tree roots do most of their work in the top 30cm (12in) or so of soil, so – contrary to previous advice – it is no longer necessary to dig down really deep. It's important, though, to incorporate as much moisture-retaining humus as possible into the topsoil because, apart from normal evaporation, the chalk beneath the surface mops up soil moisture remarkably quickly in dry weather.

Mulching the surface of the soil with good garden compost or leaf mould works wonders in keeping moisture in the soil and maintaining it in good condition. Ground cover in the form of plants is valuable too: underplant trees with drought-tolerant mat-formers such as perennial geraniums, *Vinca minor*, *Brunnera*, *Alchemilla mollis* and other tough, low-growing plants with spreading leaves that last for a long season. They not only make a pleasing tapestry of leaves and flowers, but are also a great help in preventing evaporation and keeping tree roots moist.

More trees for chalky soil

Arbutus unedo (*see* page 72)
Cercis siliquastrum (*see* page 74)
Ligustrum lucidum (*see* page 80)
Malus (*see* pages 82–3)
Morus nigra (*see* page 84)
Prunus lusitanica (*see* page 25)
Syringa (*see* page 89)

Native chalk dwellers

Once established, a carefully chosen tree on chalky soil should have little difficulty. Britain has very large areas of chalk, especially in the south, and there is no shortage of trees that thrive there – yew, box, holly, juniper, hawthorn, field maple and whitebeam, to name just a few. All of these wild trees, and more besides, have garden-worthy forms.

A hedgerow shrub native to chalky areas that also has useful garden forms and relatives is the spindle, *Euonymus europaeus*. 'Red Cascade' is a well-known spindle cultivar that makes a pleasing, bushy little tree. In spring it is hung with delicate, green flowers that later turn into extraordinary, shocking-pink fruits. These split open by autumn to reveal bright orange seeds inside. Another reason for growing 'Red Cascade' is the splendid autumn leaf colour, which explains the cultivar name. Upright varieties of *Mahonia*, though usually classed as shrubs, also work well as small trees on chalky soil. The bright yellow flowers are a cheering sight in early winter.

Recommended small trees

There are many variables to consider when choosing a tree. Most of us want one that is easy to look after and attractive to look at, and that will not outgrow its space. Personal taste can also play a big part: some people love flowering cherries or conifers, for example, while others steer well clear of them. And if you're a keen gardener, a small, sheltered plot could be your chance to try something unusual – perhaps a tree that is on the edge of hardiness. The following pages will help you to find a tree that is suitable, both for you and for the place where it is to grow.

A–Z directory

This directory includes many of the trees you are likely to see in smaller gardens. It features 'old faithfuls' that are popular and easy to grow, along with a selection of more unusual compact trees. Not all will suit the tiniest spaces: for more information on how tree size, shape and character affect suitability, *see* page 11, The trees in this book.

Abies koreana
Korean fir

Many of the silver firs make huge trees, but a good specimen of the Korean fir can be a real asset to a small garden, not only for its manageable size and architectural form but also for its eye-catching cones, which sit on the branches like stubby candles. The best ones are a deep violet-blue, and appear even on quite young trees. To be sure of a compact tree with cones of a good colour, buy your tree from a reputable nursery: *Abies koreana* is a very variable species, so a tree raised from seed from an unknown source may turn out disappointingly. A good selection will be healthy, shapely and slow-growing, reaching only 3m (10ft) or so after 10 years.

Acacia baileyana
'Purpurea'

This choice little tree is rather tender but it can succeed in mild, sheltered gardens and adapts well to being grown in a large pot. The unusual fern-like foliage of a well-grown specimen is always a talking point: the young shoots are dusky purple, maturing to a beautiful blue-grey. The whole tree becomes a rather hectic sight in early spring, when typical mimosa flowers appear – yellow, fluffy and sweetly scented. Like many slightly tender plants, it is likely to do better in well-drained soil. Be sure to stake the young tree firmly until it is well established.

Acer See pages 70–1.

Albizia julibrissin f. rosea
Silk tree

Like its relatives, the acacias, this little tree needs summer warmth to grow well, and will tolerate hot, dry conditions and even poor soil. Its exotic appearance makes it worth trying in a sunny town garden, where it will stand up well to low winter temperatures. The deep-green leaves resemble ferns but are deciduous, turning yellow before they fall. They fold up at night like those of the so-called 'sensitive plant', *Mimosa pudica*. Fluffy, pink flowers appear over several weeks in summer.

Alnus
Alder

Often seen on riverbanks and lakesides, alders are especially attractive in early spring, when the branches are festooned with both small cones and long, dangling catkins. Common alder (*Alnus glutinosa*) will eventually grow too large for a small garden, but its more delicate, cut-leaved cultivar *Alnus glutinosa* 'Imperialis' makes a fine garden tree with its feathery foliage and neater conical shape. It is best in a reasonably sheltered position. Another lovely garden alder is the golden-leaved form of the grey alder, *Alnus incana* 'Aurea'. Its orange shoots and red catkins are a cheering sight in spring, especially against a dark backdrop or where the young leaves are lit by low sunshine.

Abies koreana

Acacia baileyana '**Purpurea**'

Albizia julibrissin f. *rosea*

Alnus incana '**Aurea**'

Acer japonicum 'Aconitifolium'

Acer palmatum 'Sango-kaku'

Acer palmatum 'Bloodgood'

Acer Maples

Unlike some popular garden trees, the maples don't do spectacular clouds of blossom, but they are widely prized for their many other worthwhile attributes. As ornamental trees, maples have a head start over their rivals for their attractive leaf form – usually the familiar hand-shaped arrangement of five or more pointed lobes that can be so elegant, notably in some of the Japanese maples. This pleasing foliage gives a long season of interest, especially in the many maples that develop flamboyant autumn colours. A few hard-working maples never take time off from looking handsome, even in winter, making a valuable contribution with their beautifully coloured and textured bark.

Japanese maples

Some of the cultivars derived from *Acer palmatum* are among the most suitable maples for really small gardens. These beautiful trees and shrubs have long captured the imagination of growers and collectors, and it's now possible to list 500 different varieties. The basic needs of most are a sheltered position and moist, fertile soil that does not become waterlogged. Some are more temperamental than others, however, and for most purposes it's best to stick with the tried-and-tested few that have proved to be reliable and beautiful for a long season.

'Sango-kaku' is an excellent one to start with. Its leaves change colour through the growing season, opening orange and maturing to pale green, then becoming golden yellow in autumn. Its contribution to the garden in winter, when the pink bark is at its brightest (it is often called the coral-bark maple), gives it a further advantage over many of its competitors. This is especially true in a small garden, where it is more likely to be seen from the house. This tree has a pleasing vase-like shape and is also more lime-tolerant than some Japanese maples (but don't expect miracles on bone-dry chalk). *Acer palmatum* 'Bloodgood' also suits small spaces, with its upright habit and elegant burgundy-coloured leaves. These keep their colour well through the summer, before turning brilliant crimson in autumn. The small tree *Acer japonicum* likes similar conditions to *Acer palmatum*. It has just a handful of cultivars: 'Aconitifolium', with deeply dissected green leaves, and 'Vitifolium', with leaves like a vine, are two of the best, both taking on vivid autumn colour.

A closely related maple, also from Japan, has a most romantic English name:

the golden full-moon maple. It is *Acer shirasawanum* 'Aureum', a slow-growing small tree that produces the best leaf colour in partial shade. With a spreading canopy of lime-yellow foliage, it is a good choice for brightening a dull area and making a focal point. Each leaf is like a starburst, changing colour through the year, from pale yellow in spring to a greener yellow in summer, and then to red-flushed gold in autumn. The cultivar 'Autumn Moon' is the one to choose for late-season colour.

Maples for bark

Acer griseum, the paper-bark maple, was introduced into Britain from China by the great plant collector, E.H. Wilson. One of his favourite plants and still highly prized by many knowledgeable gardeners, it is in many ways ideal for the average-sized garden: a neat, compact tree that is easy to grow. The attractively shaped leaves and handsome bark look beautiful whatever the time of year. Even when the tree is quite young, the thinly peeling, curling bark in warm shades of russet and orange makes a winter feature when the tree is bare; in summer it contrasts attractively with the light canopy of rich-green leaves. In autumn, bark and leaves join forces in a finale of warm russet and red tones.

The snake-bark maples have interesting bark of a different kind. *Acer davidii*, from China, is grown mainly for the winter interest offered by its cream-and-green striated bark, but it is really a multi-season tree. Red buds and young leaves in spring are followed by colourful seedcases and foliage in autumn. 'George Forrest' is a widely available improved form. *Acer capillipes* is a similar snake-bark maple, from Japan; the stripy *Acer pensylvanicum* (moosewood) hails from North America.

Maples for spring and summer

Acer pseudoplatanus 'Brilliantissimum' has its moment of glory in spring, and is often snapped up in garden centres on account of its salmon-pink young foliage. This changes through shades of bronze and yellow to green by midsummer, when the tree begins to look rather dull, heavy and nondescript – a reminder that it is a sycamore at heart. Fortunately, it is a slow-growing cultivar reaching only 6–10m (20–33ft). In a medium-sized garden it can always be positioned where its off-season will not be too obvious.

A second very popular maple with striking foliage that accounts for many impulse buys is *Acer negundo* 'Flamingo'. This is a good tree for a border, where its pretty tricoloured young foliage in green, pink and white can be a great asset, and where the plant's rather gawky shape as it matures will be better disguised. It looks best of all if the branches are pollarded (*see* page 51) each winter; this not only keeps the tree compact but also allows it to make a complete head of fresh, colourful growth every year.

... and a maple for the birds

Acer campestre is the field maple, Britain's only indigenous maple and one of the best native garden trees where space is not too restricted, especially on chalk or limestone soils. It has a small version of the typical maple leaf, and is a fine sight in autumn, when the whole tree turns a buttery golden yellow. It is a particularly good wildlife tree, providing food and shelter for a wide range of insects, which in turn attract birds. The prolific crop of winged fruits appeals to seed-eating birds as well as to voles and wood mice. Any uneaten seeds may eventually germinate, so look out for seedlings around older trees: these make good hedging plants.

Acer griseum

Acer pseudoplatanus **'Brilliantissimum'**

Acer negundo 'Flamingo'

Acer campestre

Amelanchier × grandiflora 'Ballerina'

Arbutus unedo f. *rubra*

Azara microphylla

Amelanchier

If you have to choose just one tree for a small garden with reasonable soil, put an amelanchier on your shortlist. These elegant, compact trees earn their space with interest at every season, from the delicate white blossom of spring, beautifully set off by young bronze leaves, to the fiery foliage of autumn. They also fruit, bearing a summer crop of juicy black berries that birds can't resist, especially in dry weather. The names of different amelanchiers cause much confusion in the nursery trade, and they can be difficult to tell apart. *Amelanchier lamarckii* is perhaps the most popular, but you will also find *Amelanchier canadensis* and the excellent hybrid *Amelanchier × grandiflora* 'Ballerina'. All are small, spreading trees that can be pruned to give either a multi-stemmed specimen or a single trunk.

Arbutus unedo
Strawberry tree

Broadleaved evergreens are often inclined to be a little tender, and the members of the *Arbutus* group are not among the hardiest. But the comparatively tough *Arbutus unedo* is worth trying in any reasonably mild area, even on chalky or limy soil. It is especially useful in coastal gardens, appreciating the relatively even temperatures at the seaside and able to withstand salt-laden winds. A mature specimen, with its red bark glowing in low sunshine, is a beautiful sight, and the tree is quite a curiosity in autumn, when its white or pinkish flowers and strawberry-like fruits (edible, but pretty tasteless) appear at the same time. Two compact forms suited to quite tiny gardens are 'Atlantic' and 'Elfin King'. *Arbutus unedo* f. *rubra* has flowers flushed with deep pink.

Azara microphylla

Given a sheltered spot, this little-known South American evergreen will reward you every spring with wafts of a delicious scent, somewhere between vanilla and chocolate, that comes from tiny, golden flowers tucked away under the twigs. The leaves are small, so the effect is light and airy for an evergreen. Where it is happy (it tolerates partial shade) this tree grows into a slim, upright evergreen – good in Mediterranean-style gardens, or for disguising a vertical feature without cutting out light. The tree can become rather gawky as it ages.

Betula *See* opposite.

Buxus sempervirens
Box

Although it is seldom grown as a freestanding tree, box is widely used for topiary and can be invaluable in tiny spaces where a tree-like shape on a small scale is needed. It is very tolerant of both shade and dry soil, so it's a good small tree to grow beneath the canopy of larger ones. Try growing it as a 'lollipop', or 'cloud prune' it (*see* page 25) for a sculptural effect. Unlike many trees, box is very good-natured when it comes to pruning: it tolerates repeated cutting, even into mature wood, and can be fashioned into almost any shape to make a focal point or to help screen out an eyesore. Its dense foliage suits either being clipped with shears, into crisp, sharp-edged architectural shapes, or being cut with secateurs to give a more natural effect. Box blight (*see* page 57) has become a problem recently: check plants before you buy for any tell-tale signs, such as mouldy or browned leaves.

Buxus sempervirens

Betula Birches

Birches are a pleasure to look at in every month of the year: fresh in spring, golden in autumn, and valuable as winter features for their handsome bark. Most birches grow quickly and eventually become tall, but many have a rather upright growth habit, taking up far less lateral space than many trees of similar height. This means they are worth considering for all but the tiniest gardens. But don't try to adapt birches to confined spaces by pruning, as this can easily spoil their naturally graceful character.

Silver birches

One of the best native trees for gardens, especially on poor, dry soil, the silver birch (*Betula pendula*) is often dubbed the lady of the woods, reflecting its slender profile and graceful habit. With its fine twigs and fluttering, airy foliage, it never looks bulky and oppressive, even in high summer, and it casts only light shade, so quite a wide range of plants can be grown beneath it provided the soil is kept in good condition. It's also a useful tree for attracting wildlife, supporting a good population of insects, and ripening its catkins to produce countless tiny seeds that are always popular with finches and other small birds.

Several silver birch cultivars have been selected for gardens. One often recommended for small gardens is *Betula pendula* 'Youngii'. This mop-shaped tree is barely half as tall as an ordinary silver birch, but is much less graceful and takes up more ground because its low, spreading habit makes it difficult to use the space beneath: the weeping branches eventually sweep right down to the ground. A taller weeping variety is *Betula pendula* 'Tristis' (the Latin name means 'sad'). Another garden form, *Betula pendula* 'Laciniata' (often incorrectly named 'Dalecarlica'), has pretty, divided, fern-like leaves. It can make a very attractive tree but is more disease-prone than the species, *Betula pendula*, which is usually resilient.

Non-native birches

Several birches from distant parts of the world are widely grown as garden trees. The most popular, cropping up again and again in contemporary gardens (usually in multi-stemmed form), is the Himalayan birch, *Betula utilis* var. *jacquemontii*. Its gleaming white bark can look really spectacular in winter, especially when brushed and polished by enthusiastic gardeners. Most varieties grow too big for small gardens, but a more compact one is 'Grayswood Ghost'. Another birch from the Far East that is increasingly seen in winter gardens is *Betula albosinensis*, with peeling, satiny bark in warm, coppery shades, and long catkins. 'Fascination' is an especially good cultivar. The river birch, *Betula nigra*, is also a good bet, especially on damp soils, though not in very small gardens. Cultivars selected for their ornamental qualities include *Betula nigra* 'Heritage', with peeling bark, and *Betula nigra* 'Summer Cascade', for its attractive weeping habit.

Betula pendula 'Tristis'

Betula utilis var. *jacquemontii*

Planting with birches

Birches are very versatile, and are equally at home in contemporary-style gardens and wild ones. Their shallow roots make them poor companions for plants that need rich soil, but an underplanting of small woodland bulbs and tough perennials suits them well. White flowers look especially attractive under white-barked birches: try *Galium odoratum*, *Geranium macrorrhizum* 'Album' or white foxgloves (*Digitalis purpurea* f. *albiflora*).

Betula nigra 'Heritage'

Catalpa bignonioides 'Aurea'

Cercis canadensis 'Forest Pansy'

Cercis siliquastrum

Corylus avellana

Catalpa bignonioides 'Aurea'

This golden form of the Indian bean tree is worth considering where space is not too restricted, for the dramatic effect of its large, heart-shaped, golden leaves and spreading crown – a delight if it is pruned with a view to being able to sit underneath it on a hot day. An alternative treatment is to coppice the tree every year to produce a multi-stemmed plant with even larger leaves (*see* page 51). This is perfect if you want to create a jungle effect, even in a small space, and can also be achieved by planting a young tree in a large pot. Catalpas can be pollarded too. Hard-pruned plants, however, will not carry the exotic-looking, white flowers and characteristic long, thin seedpods that are produced by unpruned specimens. A hybrid, *Catalpa × erubescens* 'Purpurea', has shoots and young leaves of a dramatic deep purple-black. It can be coppiced in the same way.

Cercis canadensis 'Forest Pansy'

This was the must-have fashionable plant a few years ago, with demand always exceeding supply. Nowadays it is more widely available and it has become accepted as part of the keen gardener's repertoire, though larger specimens are sometimes rather expensive. With a compact habit, silky, translucent leaves, and dusky purple colouring that changes in autumn to countless subtle hues of bronze, gold and russet, this tree is a real winner. It needs a sheltered spot and will appreciate a well-drained soil with plenty of humus. Sometimes the leader of a young plant needs support to encourage it to grow vertically and make a good length of trunk for the mature tree.

Cercis siliquastrum
Judas tree

A Judas tree in flower is a spellbinding sight, with bright pink, stemless, pea-like flowers bursting from apparently every surface just as the leaves begin to open in late spring. But this is not a one-trick plant: its attractive, rounded leaves and pleasing, compact dome shape ensure that it earns its garden space by looking good all year. It is often grown as a multi-stemmed specimen and is ideal for a Mediterranean-style garden. The Judas tree is especially worthwhile on poor, dry soils, including chalk, where choosing the right tree can be tricky. Avoid siting it where the early-morning sun could catch the blossom after an overnight frost, or the flowers will scorch and you'll have to wait another year for the pleasure. As with many trees, flowering will be most prolific in years following warm summers, when the wood has been well ripened.

Cornus *See* opposite.

Corylus avellana
Hazel

A brilliant small native tree for a wildlife garden, hazel is ideal for creating a woodland effect where there is space for three or four plants. Thriving on regular coppicing, it can be cut to the ground every few years to allow more light to reach plants growing beneath, and new stems will spring up from the base in no time. The prunings make excellent plant supports, bean-poles and pea-sticks, and can be woven to make a low edging for borders. On older stems, the yellow catkins of early spring are a bonus, as well as fresh hazelnuts to pick in early autumn: delicious to eat before they dry out.

Cornus Dogwoods

The dogwoods can be either trees or shrubs, and with some of them the choice is yours: leave them in their naturally bushy shape or prune out the lower branches to turn them into a single-stemmed tree.

Variegated dogwoods

Cornus controversa 'Variegata' has become a very well-known tree in recent years, popular with designers of show gardens for its elegant shape with level tiers: it is sometimes called the table dogwood or wedding cake tree. The pretty, white-variegated foliage looks particularly handsome in semi-shade. It grows rather slowly but can get quite big over time. Similarly graceful but more compact is *Cornus alternifolia* 'Argentea'. This is usually thought of as a shrub, but a little artful pruning to give it a clear trunk and accentuate its tiered habit makes it a good substitute where there is no space for *Cornus controversa*. Both plants are happiest in well-drained but humus-rich soil that is not too alkaline.

Flowering dogwoods

This is a slightly strange but widely understood term used to describe a particular group of tree-like dogwoods: strange because all dogwoods flower, and because the so-called flowers on trees in this group aren't actually flowers at all. Each one is made up of the four large bracts that enclose the flower buds before they open. The bracts then open out to surround the actual flowers – which are tiny and rather insignificant – with a showy star-like device, rather like a white or pink flower. A tree covered with these in early summer is a picture indeed, and most types follow on with attractive fruits and colourful autumn foliage.

Flowering dogwoods differ from the shrubby dogwoods in another important respect: most of them dislike alkaline soil, so are not suitable for dry, chalky gardens, preferring fertile soil that is well drained but does not dry out. *Cornus* 'Porlock' is one of the best flowering dogwoods, a hybrid between *Cornus capitata* and *Cornus kousa*. Its white bracts gradually turn pink, and fruits that look slightly similar to strawberries appear later on. Other popular cultivars include *Cornus* 'Eddie's White Wonder', which colours particularly well in the autumn, the graceful *Cornus kousa* var. *chinensis*, and many forms of *Cornus florida*. Most flowering dogwoods are under 10m (33ft) tall. Some grow happily on a single stem; others do better as multi-stemmed plants.

Cornelian cherry

Cornus mas, the cornelian cherry, is sometimes seen brightening late-winter hedgerows with its bobbles of fluffy, golden flowers. Naturally a rather dense, twiggy shrub, it can be made more tree-like with pruning, and will grow to about 3m (10ft). It looks best planted in front of a dark background to show up the flowers and shiny, cherry-like, bright red fruits in autumn. Its white-variegated cultivar, *Cornus mas* 'Variegata', is more slow-growing but beautiful and makes a useful, very small variegated tree for a semi-shaded border, especially on chalky soil that is not too dry.

Planting with dogwoods

Both the flowering dogwoods and the variegated dogwoods above make fine specimen trees: they are lovely enough in their spring season not to need a supporting cast. A dark background shows them off well. For interest later in the year, consider underplanting with cyclamen or autumn crocus.

Cornus controversa '**Variegata**'

Cornus '**Porlock**'

Cornus mas

Cotoneaster 'Hybridus Pendulus'

Cupressus sempervirens

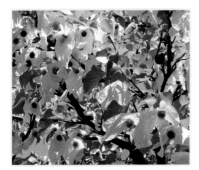

Cydonia oblonga

Davidia involucrata

Cotoneaster

There are cotoneasters in just about every shape and size and they have enjoyed enormous popularity as garden shrubs. *Cotoneaster frigidus* 'Cornubia' is among the larger and more tree-like ones, a vigorous and reliable, upright semi-evergreen that is practically guaranteed to have a good berry crop. Its growth habit is not the most refined, but this is a workhorse of a plant, to be considered if screening is needed quickly in places where growing conditions are less than ideal. A more compact cotoneaster for a decorative effect is *Cotoneaster* 'Hybridus Pendulus', which carries similar white flowers and red berries on a very small weeping tree.

Crataegus See opposite.

Cupressus sempervirens
Mediterranean cypress

No plant is more evocative of Tuscan hillsides than this very slender, elegant evergreen. Ideal conditions are the mild, wet winters and hot, dry summers that characterize a Mediterranean climate, so the plant is more likely to succeed in sheltered gardens in mild regions. Natural genetic variations mean that some forms will be hardier than others, as well as more shapely and robust, so choose a cultivar that has been tried and tested in Britain, such as 'Green Pencil'. Spring is the best time to plant, giving the trees a chance to get established before having to cope with the ups and downs of winter. Mediterranean cypress is best established as a young plant: mature specimens may be slow to establish and may never achieve a firm roothold. (They are eye-wateringly expensive, too!)

Cydonia oblonga
Quince

Often overlooked for garden use because it falls between a fruit tree and an ornamental plant, this native of central Asia is easy to grow and can make an unusual and lovely feature in reasonably sheltered gardens, though the fruits may not ripen every year. The flowers, of palest pink, open in spring from exquisite spiralled buds. The ripe yellow fruits, usually roughly pear-shaped and sometimes as large as a grapefruit, are highly aromatic both on the tree in autumn and after picking, when just one fruit can fill a room with its unique aroma. For best results buy a named variety: 'Meech's Prolific' (a reliable cropper) and 'Vranja' are among the hardiest.

Davidia involucrata
Handkerchief tree

This iconic tree from China was the Holy Grail of 19th-century plant hunters, and was finally introduced to Britain in 1901. The common name is explained by the pairs of floating white bracts that frame each of the tiny, dark flower clusters: the effect of looking up into the tree in its spring flowering season is mesmerizing. The bracts gradually fade to green, blending in with the attractive heart-shaped leaves. The fruits – hanging spherical bobbles – keep the tree looking interesting right into winter. Also called the dove tree and the ghost tree, davidia is a tree for patient enthusiasts, taking ten years or so to reach flowering size. But if your aim is to plant something really special for posterity, this could be the answer – provided you are not looking for a tiny tree for a tiny space and, because it prefers moist, rich ground, you have reasonable soil that is not too dry.

Crataegus Hawthorns

A windswept site or thin, dry soil are all in a day's work for wild hawthorns, which flower and fruit reliably in even the most grim places. While their cultivated cousins may be a little less phlegmatic, they are likely to do much better than many fussier trees in inhospitable sites, being good all-rounders and one of the best groups of trees for tolerating poor conditions. Many of these trees are naturally armed, so remember not to plant the thornier varieties too close to a path or a seat.

Native hawthorns

The common hawthorn (*Crataegus monogyna*) is seen in gardens as a hedge more often than as a tree, though its spectacular froth of heady cream blossom, its prolific crop of autumn haws and its attractiveness to wildlife certainly make it a good candidate for a natural garden. And it is simplicity itself to grow. It has a number of cultivars but they are not well known, unlike those of the other native, the Midland hawthorn. *Crataegus laevigata* 'Paul's Scarlet' is the most popular of the Midland's cultivars, and produces deep pinkish-red double flowers. It is seriously showy for a short period in spring, but unremarkable for the rest of the year, with neither fruit nor

autumn colour. *Crataegus laevigata* 'Crimson Cloud' is a much better bet, with more delicate, single deep-pink flowers that have a white centre, while 'Gireoudii' has cream-mottled leaves and typical creamy hawthorn blossom; both bear red fruits in autumn.

Hawthorns from elsewhere

A more unusual hawthorn that is ideal for small gardens is *Crataegus orientalis*, also sometimes known as *Crataegus laciniata*. Compact and shapely, it has prettily divided leaves that are silvery underneath, typical hawthorn blossom and large ornamental fruits. *Crataegus tanacetifolia*, though harder to find, is a gem. Its fern-like leaves are even more silvery, the fruits are yellow and the tree is usually thornless. Both these attractive little trees are from south-eastern Europe and Asia.

Several hawthorns found in gardens have oval leaves, rather than the typical ragged, lobed leaves of wild hawthorns. *Crataegus crus-galli* is known as the cockspur thorn with good reason, for its thorns are spectacularly huge. The large fruits ripen to a bold bright red and usually stay on the tree into the new year, looking splendid with a backdrop of clear winter sky – until they are found by birds. The cockspur thorn is the parent of a hybrid thorn that is one of the best garden varieties: *Crataegus × lavalleei* 'Carrierei'. This has a more upright shape and larger orange-red fruits, and is good value for screening as it keeps its leaves until early winter. It also flowers rather later than most hawthorns. A similar tree, which may also be related to the cockspur thorn, is *Crataegus persimilis* 'Prunifolia'. Its thorns are smaller than the cockspur's, but it has the same spreading habit. The leaves turn rich-red shades in autumn, and the red berries are usually plentiful.

Planting with hawthorns

A cloud of white May blossom looks wonderful alone or with almost any other plants. Cow parsley (*Anthriscus sylvestris*) is a classic companion for a meadow or woodland feel, perhaps studded with the dazzling blue bulb *Camassia quamash*. The scarlet autumn berries make hawthorns a good backdrop for late-season hot colours, such as dahlias and penstemons, and shrubs with bronze or purple foliage.

Crataegus monogyna

Crataegus laevigata '**Crimson Cloud**'

Crataegus × lavalleei '**Carrierei**'

Eucalyptus gunnii

Eucryphia × nymansensis 'Nymansay'

Ficus carica

Genista aetnensis

Eucalyptus

Most eucalyptus trees are too vigorous and large for a small garden and not all are very hardy, but sometimes their glaucous evergreen foliage and attractive bark may be just what is needed. A good compromise is to grow *Eucalyptus gunnii*, the cider gum, and cut back all or part of the plant really hard each spring. This will both control its size and give a continuing supply of juvenile leaves, which are a lovely silver-blue colour and attractively rounded – unlike the leaves on older wood. It can either be grown on a 'leg' to form a mop-headed tree, or cut at ground level. A newish, more compact cultivar, *Eucalyptus gunnii* 'Azura', is hardier and bushier than the species. Another possibility is the compact *Eucalyptus pauciflora* subsp. *niphophila*, the snow gum, which has peeling, whitish-grey bark. Always establish eucalyptus when it is young, and avoid pot-bound plants: older specimens often fail to root firmly.

Eucryphia

A little out of the ordinary, eucryphias makes good specimen trees in a limited space because of their columnar habit. Many dislike lime, but the vigorous, semi-evergreen hybrid *Eucryphia × nymansensis* 'Nymansay' can cope with alkaline soils as long as they are not too dry. In a cool, sheltered position, with plenty of leaf mould added to the soil, it should reward you year after year in late summer with abundant honey-scented flowers, white with red or pink stamens and always alive with bees. *Eucryphia × intermedia* 'Rostrevor' is a fine evergreen with a longer flowering season, but it does need acid soil. So too does *Eucryphia glutinosa*, a deciduous form whose leaves turn a glorious orange-red in autumn.

Ficus carica
Fig

Whether grown for its fruit or its large, deeply divided, architectural leaves, a fig tree gives a garden a comfortable, settled look – maybe because ancient specimens are often associated with old gardens in warmer climates. Figs are undemanding, easy plants, tolerating poor soil when established, though they fruit better in a sheltered, sunny spot. A fig is an ideal small tree to grow in a large container on a warm patio, but don't let it go short of food or water, especially if you want fruit. The branches of fig trees tend to become lanky, but can be controlled by pruning. Many varieties can be bought from specialist nurseries, but for hardiness and reliability the widely available 'Brown Turkey' is probably the best. On a warm, sunny wall you might try a more choice, extra-sweet cultivar such as 'Rouge de Bordeaux' or 'White Marseilles'.

Genista aetnensis
Mount Etna broom

A Mount Etna broom in full flower in high summer makes a fine showpiece for a dry, sunny garden – as long as space is not really limited. The great fountain of sweetly scented, golden-yellow flowers is glorious if you can organize a clear blue sky behind it, but also uplifting on a dull day. Although this is quite a bulky tree, it has a light and airy texture and casts little shade. It's wise to thin the plant as it grows, to help develop a single strong trunk and a good shape. Low branches are best cut out at the base, raising the crown to give room for planting beneath the canopy. Native to the hills of Sardinia and Sicily, it's a natural partner for sun-loving plants such as lavender, sages and other low-growing aromatic shrubs.

Gleditsia triacanthos
Honey locust

'Sunburst' is a deservedly popular form of the honey locust. It is not suitable for really tiny spaces, but elsewhere it is a fine choice for golden foliage. Its small, fern-like leaves and light canopy won't easily shade out other plants growing beneath it. For the brightest golden colouring, plant the tree in full sun – though the foliage does tend to lose its brightness and become increasingly green in summer. This tree tolerates a wide range of soil types. 'Rubylace' is a smaller honey locust cultivar, and has deep-red leaves that change to bronze as they mature. It's an unusual, compact tree, and worth trying where adjacent colours will suit it. A mixed border will often make a good setting for both its colour and its habit.

Ilex aquifolium and Ilex × altaclerensis
Holly

Holly is valuable as a tree or a shrub for small gardens, suiting various soils and situations. It tolerates repeated clipping or pruning, whether to shape it as a structural plant or to control its size. The glossy, distinctively shaped leaves and the red berries ensure that it never becomes oppressive like some other evergreens do. Both the native Ilex aquifolium and the hybrid Ilex × altaclerensis have numerous variegated cultivars. Female clones (some with confusing 'male' names such as Ilex × altaclerensis 'Golden King') will produce berries if there is a male plant within range; the cultivar Ilex aquifolium 'J.C. van Tol', however, is self-fertile. A word of warning: look out for holly leaf blight, a fungal disease that causes black blotches on the leaves followed by leaf drop and dieback on the stems. Unfortunately, there is no treatment other than cutting out and destroying any infected leaves and shoots.

Juniperus
Juniper

Although usually thought of as a shrub, juniper comes in a host of shapes and sizes, and some of its many cultivars grow into quite large trees. Others are compact, but tree-like in their effect, and these are the most useful in small spaces. The British native Juniperus communis can take on a variety of shapes according to the cultivar. Slender, upright forms, such as Juniperus communis 'Hibernica' (Irish juniper) and 'Sentinel', come into their own in restricted spaces, especially on poor alkaline soils: juniper grows in the wild on chalk and limestone. Juniperus scopulorum 'Skyrocket' is another very slim cultivar that is widely available.

Koelreuteria paniculata
Golden-rain tree

This unusual tree makes a very good specimen in sunny, well-drained gardens with space to accommodate its spreading crown. The large and attractive pinnate leaves are pinkish red when young, and the strange but rather pretty coral-tinged, bladder-like seedpods are an autumn feature. The tree's moment of glory comes in high summer, when its swags of bright yellow flowers appear. Especially abundant in warm summers, they are memorable when brought to life by low sunlight. Koelreuteria is easy to propagate from either seed or cuttings, and the offspring can be used equally well as shrubs, producing even larger leaves if pruned hard when young.

Gleditsia triacanthos '**Rubylace**'

Ilex × altaclerensis '**Golden King**'

Juniperus communis '**Sentinel**'

Koelreuteria paniculata

Laburnum × watereri 'Vossii'

Laurus nobilis

Ligustrum lucidum 'Excelsum Superbum'

Luma apiculata

Laburnum

Laburnum is among the most familiar of all garden trees, grown solely for its star turn in late spring, when the tree becomes a mass of hanging bunches of yellow flowers. It is often seen trained over arches and tunnels, making one of the set-piece garden spectacles. The cultivar to grow is *Laburnum × watereri* 'Vossii'. It has the showiest flowers and, importantly, it does not develop the pea-like, very poisonous seedpods that make laburnums such a hazard where small children are playing. Laburnum is easy to grow but its rather gawky habit makes it tricky to keep compact by pruning, so plant it only where it will not have to be constrained in this way.

Laurus nobilis
Sweet bay

One of the best evergreens for a sunny garden, bay is a good-natured plant and can be pruned and trained to fit even the smallest space, either as a 'lollipop' tree or with foliage down to the ground in a cone or pyramid. When you shape the plant, use secateurs and leave the individual leaves intact; shears will result in sharp cut edges that spoil the natural habit of the bush and sometimes turn an ugly brown. Pruned specimens

Fragrant trees

Many trees contribute a very special and subtle magic to the garden with their perfume. Some – such as sweet bay, pines, eucalyptus and myrtles – have aromatic foliage. Others have scented flowers; frequently these are tiny and inconspicuous, for example those of *Azara microphylla* or *Pittosporum tenuifolium*. Position these trees where sunshine will waft the fragrance into the warm air – and ideally alongside a seat or a path that you use regularly, where the scent is sure to take you by surprise.

need regular feeding and watering, especially when they are grown in containers. Watch out for scale insects on the stems and leaves and rub them off if you see them.

Ligustrum lucidum 'Excelsum Superbum'
Variegated Chinese privet

Evergreen trees with variegated foliage are few and far between, but this variegated privet is particularly useful in that it combines permanent screening with a lighter, airier look than solid green leaves. It is also less vigorous than the species. Like many broadleaved evergreens, this handsome privet is not a plant for really cold places, but in a sheltered garden with well-drained soil it can be just the job. The large leaves catch the light with their broad margin of creamy yellow, and the sprays of white flowers develop slowly until the early autumn, when the buds open to release their fragrance.

Luma apiculata

This South American relative of myrtle (it is sometimes called *Myrtus luma*) has long been a feature of the mild, damp coastal gardens of the West Country and Ireland, where the peeling, warm-orange bark of the mature tree sings out in contrast with the small, neat, dark green leaves. Now, climate change is allowing this tree to succeed over a wider area, and it is well worth a try in sheltered, sunny gardens where the soil is well drained but does not dry out. The starry, creamy-white flowers in late summer each have a fuzz of long stamens, like those of the common myrtle, and the black berries are similar to those of myrtle too.

Magnolia

Magnolias take some beating if 'wow factor' is your aim. These beautiful flowering plants were among the prize finds of early plant hunters, who over the years brought back more than 100 species from far-flung regions of both the Far East and America. Growers and keen gardeners ever since have delighted in raising numerous cultivars and hybrids, both evergreen and deciduous, and in sizes and shapes ranging from huge trees to compact shrubs that will suit all but the smallest of gardens.

Magnolia cultivars

Many magnolias grow too large for small gardens, and most (but not all) are intolerant of alkaline soil. If you are unsure about a particular cultivar – care, pruning requirements or suitability – a specialist nursery should be able to advise you. These are plants with a justifiably enthusiastic following, and much detailed knowledge of individual cultivars is out there. You just need to know where to look: the Internet makes this very easy.

Reliable, beautiful and popular, the hybrid *Magnolia* 'Heaven Scent' is a good choice if you want a pink magnolia. The scent referred to in its name is reminiscent of lavender. Needing fertile, humus-rich soil that is neutral to acid, it will eventually make a small to medium-sized, rounded tree that is always a talking point in spring when its large, elegant, vase-shaped flowers are at the peak of their performance.

Magnolia × *loebneri* cultivars can be grown either as shrubs or as bushy, single-stemmed trees, and they have some tolerance of alkaline soil. The well-known cultivar 'Leonard Messel' has white flowers that are flushed with purplish pink on the outside, giving an overall impression of pale pink. Although quite vigorous, it is compact enough for a smallish space, and even young plants will flower well. Another similar cultivar, 'Merrill', is more upright and more vigorous, with white flowers.

Lime-tolerant magnolias

With its charmingly raggedy, white flowers and compact habit, *Magnolia stellata* (star magnolia) is one of the most familiar magnolias, partly because it is easy to recognize and also partly because it is more widespread than many others, having some tolerance of alkaline soil provided it is not too dry. It is more frequently seen as a shrub than a tree, and its habit is undoubtedly more shrub-like. 'Waterlily' is a star magnolia cultivar that has delicate shell-pink flowers. The star magnolia's grey, silky flower buds, on bare branches, are an attractive feature all winter.

Even more tolerant of alkaline soils than *Magnolia stellata* is the Japanese *Magnolia kobus*, a versatile small to medium-sized tree with beautiful, large white flowers. It can take some years to settle down to maximum flowering, but is ideal for patient gardeners who have no plans to move house, or for those happy to plant for posterity.

The flowers of *Magnolia salicifolia* are smaller but otherwise rather similar to those of *Magnolia kobus*. The leaves are narrower, resembling the leaves of willow (*Salix*), as the name suggests. The most widely grown cultivar is the free-flowering 'Wada's Memory', a graceful, conical tree with upswept branches. Its scented, white flowers are similar in form to those of *Magnolia stellata*, with strap-like petals.

Magnolia kobus

Magnolia 'Heaven Scent'

Magnolia stellata

Malus × zumi 'Golden Hornet'

Malus × robusta 'Red Sentinel'

Malus transitoria

Autumn fruits

The best fruiting tree to choose will depend on whether you want crab apples that make the tastiest, most colourful jelly, or those that are the most ornamental and last longest on the tree. For persistent, handsome fruit, *Malus × robusta* 'Red Sentinel' is a good choice. An elegant, weeping but compact little tree, it looks graceful in spring, when it is covered with pink buds and white flowers, and also in autumn and winter, when the glossy, deep-scarlet fruits continue to decorate the bare branches for many weeks. 'Red Sentinel' also works well in a patio pot, and is as robust and disease-resistant as its name suggests. *Malus × scheideckeri* 'Red Jade' is another crab apple that will help to keep a small garden cheerful well into winter, with its glossy, cherry-like, bright red fruits. The tree has a pleasing umbrella shape. *Malus* 'Sun Rival' is similar but smaller and more disease-resistant.

Varieties with yellow crab apples make a splendid show when the fruit display is set ablaze by low autumn sunshine. *Malus × zumi* 'Golden Hornet' is the most popular, with blush-white, sweetly scented flowers like apple blossom, and a prolific crop of smallish, deep-yellow fruits on a compact tree. However, if birds have not stripped the tree by late autumn it can become a sorry sight, because the fruits tend to brown and rot in cold weather. A more distinguished alternative that is seen less often is the beautiful *Malus transitoria*. One of the daintiest crab apples, this has elegant, slender leaves and a mass of fragrant, white flowers on arching branches. The fruits are tiny but abundant and golden yellow, bringing a splash of sunshine to the autumn garden even on the dullest days. *Malus transitoria* is not very tall, but it is a rather spreading

Malus Crab apples

There is a bewildering variety of crab apples and many make shapely and attractive trees that are easy to grow. They flower later than most cherries and plums, and also make useful pollinators for apple trees. If you are considering a crab apple for a small garden, don't be beguiled by glossy pictures of glorious blossom alone. It will certainly look ravishing for a week or two – almost all crab apples look pleasing in flower – but make sure you choose a compact tree that earns its keep in a small space with other, more lasting features of interest: a neat shape; attractive foliage, maybe; and best of all a plentiful supply of glowing fruits to brighten the autumn garden or turn into sparkling jars of crab-apple jelly for the winter.

tree. Where space is tight, *Malus* 'Van Eseltine' may be more suitable. It has an upright habit and its rather stiff branches carry semi-double pink flowers and small, red-flushed yellow fruits.

For crab-apple jelly, one of the best varieties is *Malus* 'John Downie', widely agreed to produce the best fruits. In some ways it is more like an apple tree than many of the crab apples, with large, blush-white flowers opening from pink buds. The orange-red, oval, fleshy fruits are handsome but do not last long on the tree. If you don't use these for making jelly, the birds will certainly appreciate them as the weather grows colder.

Foliage varieties

Crab apples seldom make the grade for their foliage alone. The large group of purple-leaved cultivars contains many varieties with leaves that look lovely on opening in spring but soon become at best dull and nondescript, and at worst disfigured by disease. Most also have dark fruits that do not show up very well. So for purple foliage you may do better to look elsewhere, though *Malus* 'Directeur Moerlands' is disease-resistant, and certainly an improvement on the ever-popular but rather disappointing *Malus* × *moerlandsii* 'Profusion'. 'Directeur Moerlands' has wine-red, slightly scented flowers, set among coppery-crimson leaves. Its spring floral display is followed by deep-red fruits; like the leaves, these are held on red stalks.

Malus trilobata, an interesting and less well-known species of crab apple, is remarkable for its unusual lobed leaves that are more like a maple's. Its upright shape and rather symmetrical outline help make this tree suitable for limited spaces. It does not fruit reliably but makes up for this when its foliage changes to

bright red in autumn – quite unusual for a crab apple, though *Malus* 'Evereste' does colour well too.

Good all-rounders

Malus 'Evereste' is a reliable and pretty tree, capturing all the charm of an old cottage-garden apple tree when its abundant fragrant, white flowers open from their deep-pink buds. They eventually turn into orange-red fruits like miniature apples, which stay intact for many weeks until they are discovered by hungry birds or are gathered for jelly.

The Japanese crab apple, *Malus floribunda*, has an arching habit and is obligingly free-flowering, with dense masses of dainty, pale-pink flowers opening from crimson buds. The yellowish fruits are small and not showy, but they do give the tree a change in character later in the season. Another Far Eastern species, *Malus hupehensis* is taller than many garden forms. As a young tree, it is upright with ascending branches, but it becomes more spreading with age. Its fragrant, white flowers appear a little later than those of most apples and crab apples, so it is useful for extending the blossom season, but less so for pollinating apple trees. The foliage is top-notch, and the fruits are long-lasting, small and cherry-red.

Planting with crab apples

A crab can cover quite a spectrum of colours in its season, from delicate pinks and whites in spring to exciting reds, oranges and yellows as the fruits ripen. With clever companion planting, crabs can be invaluable in changing the mood of a garden to create stimulating seasonal variety. Purple foliage is especially complementary to crabs in all their guises: try shrubs such as purple pittosporums, Japanese maples or *Sambucus nigra* 'Black Lace' and, for underplanting, heucheras and ajugas.

Malus 'John Downie'

Malus trilobata

Malus 'Evereste'

Malus hupehensis

Mespilus germanica

Morus nigra

Olea europaea

Osmanthus × burkwoodii

Mespilus germanica
Medlar

Rather like outsize brown rose hips, medlars are most peculiar fruits and edible only when they are partly rotten, or 'bletted': the flesh then takes on something of the flavour of caramel. But whether or not you fancy eating these rather quaint fruits, the pleasingly shaped little tree makes a handsome garden feature and is very easy to grow. The foliage turns to beautiful shades of russet and gold in autumn, and after leaf fall the fruits continue to hang on the bare, rather pendulous branches, making an unusual feature well into winter.

Morus nigra
Black mulberry

This handsome tree is often regarded as rather special. While it may eventually get too large and spreading for a really small garden, it grows slowly and makes a fine centrepiece for a fair-sized lawn or open, sunny area of a garden with fertile, well-drained soil. The leaves are shiny and heart-shaped or three-lobed, and the long, raspberry-like fruits change from red to almost black when ripe. They are delicious, and positively explode with deep-red juice. This makes them very messy, readily staining paving, clothes and children's skin: a mulberry scrumper will always be found out!

Olea europaea
Olive

This classic evergreen, especially the wonderful gnarled specimens that are often hundreds of years old, symbolizes everything we love about Mediterranean regions. Something iconic about the olive has increasingly made it a 'must-have' for sheltered gardens in Britain, especially with the warming climate improving its chances of success. Olive trees now bring a touch of Mediterranean sun to countless sheltered gardens and courtyards, growing either in the ground or in large containers. They grow quickly and can be trimmed into more formal shapes or allowed to grow naturally as a bush or small standard tree, though hard pruning from time to time is a good idea to encourage a bushier plant. They are hardier than you may expect, even if a hard winter may temporarily kill off the foliage. Will you get ripe olives? Probably not, though it's possible in a mild garden.

Osmanthus × burkwoodii

Belonging to a group normally thought of as bushy shrubs, this small-leaved hybrid can, nevertheless, be turned into a charming tree. Simply prune out the lower shoots to make an elegant, small evergreen that will have an air of maturity after only a few years' growth. The fragrant, white blossom is a bonus, showing up well against the dark foliage; you can pick sprigs of it, along with other early flowers, to bring a breath of spring indoors. Osmanthus can also be clipped into fairly formal shapes, but do this in spring, after flowering, to ensure there are plenty of flowering shoots for the following year.

Unusual fruit trees

Medlars, mulberries and quinces have long been grown in gardens. A warming climate, helped by conservatories for overwintering tender pot plants, has widened the choice of unusual fruit trees for adventurous gardeners. Crops may be patchy, but in mild gardens pomegranates, olives, loquats and citrus fruits are all possible – and pleasing to look at even if fruit is elusive.

Parrotia persica
Persian ironwood

A relative of witch hazel and with similar leaves, the Persian ironwood is grown mainly for its reliably spectacular autumn foliage. Starting early, at the shoot-tips, the colour develops into a blaze of crimson, purple and gold that lasts for several weeks. It is a rather low, spreading tree with near-horizontal branches. Drought-tolerant and able to cope with chalk or limestone, it is not, however, suitable for the smallest plots, though the cultivar 'Vanessa' has a more upright habit. But it grows slowly and, if there is space, deserves consideration as a lawn specimen or at the top of a bank where its pleasing shape, together with its tiny late-winter flowers and attractive bark, can be appreciated. The bark flakes into colourful patterns of green, orange, cream and grey, making a notable winter feature. The lower branches of the young tree can be pruned out, if necessary, to ensure a good length of colourful trunk.

Photinia × fraseri 'Red Robin'

Familiar as a shrub, 'Red Robin' is being grown more and more as a standard, making a small broadleaved evergreen tree to suit even the tiniest space. It is easy to grow and to keep pruned to size, and trimming promotes the feature for which most people buy this form – its bright red young shoots. It is perfect in 'hot' colour schemes, or as an accent among greens, but be careful not to plant it where the red spring shoots will upset an existing subtle colour scheme. And be warned that if you forget the pruning you will soon have a large, vigorous shrub on your hands! Growing it in a large container is a possible option.

Pinus pinea
Stone pine

Like many other pines, the stone pine can ultimately grow very large, but the neatly umbrella-shaped young trees look perfect in the Mediterranean-style gardens that mimic their natural habitat. Stone pines are well adapted to coastal gardens and tolerate poor, dry soils such as sand and gravel. They are the source of pine nuts (kernels), though you are unlikely to find the cones that bear these edible seeds on a tree that is less than about 20 years old. Other pines to suit more restricted spaces include the many compact or very slow-growing cultivars of the Scots pine. Those listed as *Pinus sylvestris* Fastigiata Group make attractive trees with a narrow, upright shape. For more choices, ask specialist nurseries – they will usually be happy to offer advice.

Pittosporum tenuifolium

Pittosporums are more often seen as shrubs than as trees, but this useful evergreen from New Zealand will often serve very well as a tree in all but the coldest gardens, whether grown as a column of foliage or pruned when young to give either a single unbranched trunk or several bare stems. The wavy-edged, shiny, rather delicate-looking leaves are always attractive, even in the hardier plain-green species, where they contrast prettily with the fine blackish stems. Many of the cultivars with more ornamental variegated, golden or purple foliage are more shrub-like, slower-growing and less tough, but even the most tender are well suited to mild coastal gardens or to sheltered plots in towns, where their very fragrant, tiny, maroon flowers are more likely to be appreciated in late spring.

Parrotia persica

Photinia × fraseri 'Red Robin'

Pinus pinea

Pittosporum tenuifolium

Prunus 'Accolade'

Prunus 'Shirotae'

Prunus 'Amanogawa'

Prunus Flowering cherries

Cherry blossom is an essential part of the rite of spring, with clouds of pink and white taking over parks, gardens and streets up and down the country. Some flowering cherries are very well adapted to small gardens, others less so. Certain popular garden varieties have been selected with multi-seasonal interest in mind, so that a single tree earns its space with autumn foliage colour as well as spring blossom. And some cherries continue to keep up appearances in the shortest days, with attractive bark that glows in low winter sunshine. Shape and size are important too: the big, spreading trees of old have been joined by newer cultivars that have a more upright shape and are less vigorous. A third important consideration is resistance to disease. Plums and cherries seem to be increasingly susceptible to canker and other disfiguring conditions, so it's worth selecting one of the more resilient varieties.

Japanese cherries

The Japanese passion for showy blossom has given us dozens of very ornamental flowering cherries, some of which date back many centuries. These large-flowered varieties may be fleeting in blossom but for sheer spectacle they are hard to beat – though not all suit small gardens. The white-flowered Mount Fuji cherry, *Prunus* 'Shirotae', is a favourite, with semi-double, fragrant, white flowers on a spreading but small tree. *Prunus* 'Ukon' is also quite compact, easy to grow, and has beautiful semi-double, creamy-white flowers that are flushed with green. The opening leaves are a warm coppery colour and the foliage is also a feature in autumn, when it takes on shades of gold and red.

Pink-flowering cherries, however, need careful placing, as they can make an unpleasantly clashing mix with daffodils and other spring yellows. But in the right position, trees like the one usually known as Cheal's weeping cherry (*Prunus* 'Kiku-shidare-zakura') can look a picture. This has become a garden classic, though its moment of glory is short-lived and some may find its dense pink bunches of heavy, double blossom rather too blowsy.

For smaller gardens, cherries with a columnar shape are very valuable. *Prunus* 'Amanogawa' has been called the 'flagpole cherry' with good reason: in mid-spring it is a column of scented, semi-double, pink blossom. A similar cherry but rather more tightly upright in form, the robust *Prunus* 'Spire' was selected with small gardens and street planting in mind. It has proved very popular for its semi-double, soft-pink spring flowers and autumn colour, as well as its manageable size.

Mountain cherries

Many flowering cherries are rather more modest in their appeal than the dramatic large-flowered types. Japanese gardeners call these trees, with their subtler flowers, mountain cherries – as opposed to the more showy garden cherries. *Prunus × subhirtella* 'Autumnalis' is one with an amazingly long season, opening its dainty, blush-white, semi-double flowers a few at a time from late autumn until spring. Open flowers may be spoilt by frost, but the buds escape damage so there are always more waiting in the wings. This small, slow-growing tree is perfect for small gardens, though it sometimes falls prey to disease.

Another tree with delicate flowers in very early spring is the Fuji cherry, *Prunus incisa*. Its shrubby, dwarf cultivar 'Kojo-no-mai' is widely available, but the species and its cultivars 'February Pink' and the white, early-flowering 'Praecox' are also worth trying. These are tough but dainty, densely branched little trees, with small leaves that colour well in autumn as a bonus.

Prunus cerasifera 'Nigra' has always been one of the most popular of several purple-leaved flowering cherries. It is a glorious sight in early spring, with delicate, pink-flushed blossoms and emerging dark leaves. These keep their colour quite well through the season, though the purple foliage can look a bit oppressive by midsummer. However, it does make a wonderful foil for vivid, hot colours, and choosing stimulating summer companions – for example red roses and scarlet dahlias – is a good way to bring out the best in the tree. *Prunus cerasifera* 'Spring Glow' is a more compact cherry-plum cultivar, with long-lasting, bronze leaves and vivid pink, single flowers in early spring.

Cherries for autumn colour

Prunus sargentii is an old favourite, not least for its early autumn foliage that briefly turns deep-crimson and orange, showing up well against the rather dark, banded bark. It also has abundant single, pink flowers and young bronze foliage in spring. Its more columnar and compact cultivar 'Rancho' is a better bet where space is tight. *Prunus sargentii* is a parent of the excellent hybrid *Prunus* 'Accolade' (*see* opposite), which bears delicate, semi-double, pale pink flowers on a fairly small tree that colours well in autumn. *Prunus* 'Pandora' has interesting leaf colour in both autumn and spring. It forms a neat, upright shape, with early flowers opening pale pink from deep-pink buds and fading to white. *Prunus* 'Kursar' is similar in size and also has good foliage, but the blossom is a deeper pink, while *Prunus* 'Shizuka' (also known as 'Fragrant Cloud') has white flowers that become pinkish with age, leaves that turn orange in autumn, and a lovely scent that justifies its popular name.

... and for bark

In winter, especially, trees with beautiful bark are invaluable. The best cherries among these are *Prunus serrula*, with shiny, coppery-brown, peeling bark, and *Prunus maackii* 'Amber Beauty', with bark that peels to reveal smooth, golden patches. Both are fairly compact, and both look fantastic in winter sunshine, especially when you polish the bark with a gloved hand or a soft brush or cloth.

Prunus × subhirtella 'Autumnalis'

Prunus cerasifera 'Nigra'

Prunus 'Pandora'

Prunus serrula

Pyrus calleryana '**Chanticleer**'

Pyrus salicifolia '**Pendula**'

Robinia × *slavinii* '**Hillieri**'

Pyrus calleryana 'Chanticleer'

Widely used in streets and landscaping projects, this ornamental pear has a neat, upright shape, attractive foliage and a pleasing tendency to look the picture of health. Other qualities that make it a good garden tree include its drought tolerance and the ease with which it establishes in a wide range of soils. It has the advantage of a fairly short period of bare branches, a bonus when used as a screening tree. A generous display of beautiful white pear blossom opens from silvery buds quite early in spring, and the leaves, which take on good autumn colours, usually stay on the branches until early winter. The fruits are insignificant and, sadly, not edible like their orchard cousins – but you can't have everything!

Pyrus salicifolia 'Pendula'
Weeping silver-leaved pear

This dainty tree is seen in gardens everywhere, and with good reason. Its hanging wands of slender, silver-backed leaves make a flattering 'cottagey' backdrop to classic plants such as roses, clematis and delphiniums. Fine, white down on the young leaves lends them an even more silvery effect. The tree looks particularly attractive beside water, and makes a good specimen either in a bed or in a lawn. The spreading, mop-like crown can eventually take up rather a lot of space, but careful pruning and thinning of the shoots can help to keep it within bounds. However, as with most weeping trees, the branches tend to hang down to the ground, so it is not an ideal choice if you want to be able to use the space underneath. Weeping pears can also be clipped into formal shapes and even make an attractive hedge.

Robinia

The false acacia (*Robinia pseudoacacia*) is tempting to grow for its pretty foliage and fragrant flowers, but its fast growth, large size and brittle branches make it unsuitable for small gardens. Its less vigorous cultivar 'Frisia' is often seen in town gardens, where its bright yellow foliage makes it conspicuous from some distance away. But its colouring is too strident to be suitable everywhere, and in recent years many mature specimens have begun to show signs of a decline that has not yet been explained. The mop-headed *Robinia pseudoacacia* 'Umbraculifera' is becoming quite a popular garden tree, and a compact pink-flowered robinia well suited to confined spaces is *Robinia* × *slavinii* 'Hillieri'. Prettily shaped with the typical attractive acacia-like leaves, it is a good choice for a small, sheltered garden.

Salix caprea 'Kilmarnock'
Kilmarnock willow

Many willows are too vigorous and their roots too rampant for a confined space. Never, ever plant a weeping willow in anything but a large garden, and keep it well away from house and drains. That said, not all willows are monsters. The popular Kilmarnock willow is a miniature 'manufactured' version of the native goat or pussy willow. It is a tiny, weeping tree, producing soft, silvery catkins very early in spring, just like those of its large, wild counterpart. When they develop their golden, pollen-rich anthers, the catkins become irresistible to bees. A young plant works well in a pot, and can easily be moved to a less prominent spot when its spring fling is over. Pruning as the catkins fade will help keep it neat. However, this isn't a tree that will grow old gracefully.

Salix caprea '**Kilmarnock**'

Salix exigua
Coyote willow

The words 'willow' and 'small garden' should seldom be mentioned in the same breath, but worthy exceptions include this slim, graceful North American willow, which can be a real asset in a restricted space. In the sandy soil and sunny conditions that suit it best, the coyote willow is an effective tree or tree-like shrub for lending height to a border. It casts little shade and provides a sense of lightness and movement with its slender, flexible branches and narrow, silvery leaves. If the coyote willow grows well for you, you're on to a winner!

Salix integra
'Hakuro-nishiki'

There are a few garden plants whose party-trick is to produce novel tricoloured foliage and this Japanese willow is a popular one, making a small, mop-headed tree with leaves of white and green, on pink-tipped shoots. It is appreciated most where its foliage is seen at close range, and will in turn appreciate the shelter of a courtyard or other small garden. It is a good little tree to grow in a container. Like most willows, it does not object to pruning, and is best pollarded to keep it to size and to encourage it to produce the young reddish-tinted shoots that make a winter feature after leaf fall. Any variegated plant is less robust than a plant with a fully functioning set of green leaves, but this one is particularly sensitive. Exposure or disease can disfigure the foliage, and the plant may also be short-lived. Enjoy it for a while – but don't get too attached to it!

Sorbus See pages 90–1.

Syringa
Lilac

Lilacs are usually thought of as shrubs, but the plants tend to take on a tree-like quality in middle age, and it is not difficult to shape a younger plant into a multi-stemmed tree with an umbrella of foliage and flowers. Ageing stems take on a gnarled quality that can quite quickly make a lilac tree look interestingly old and 'cottagey', and the sight and scent of a well-shaped lilac in full bloom are among the bright spots of late spring. Lilacs thrive on chalky soil and indeed flower better if not too richly fed, but they should not be allowed to dry out when young. Prune after flowering if possible.

Taxus baccata
Yew

No tree is more versatile than the native yew: the species includes Britain's most ancient trees as well as the trendiest topiary specimens. Despite being poisonous, yew is an obliging garden plant. It adds structure, is easy to grow on well-drained soil (and less slow than people often think), drought-tolerant, and also not averse to being clipped or pruned, however old the plant. This means it can be a tree of any size you choose – so if you inherit an overgrown yew hedge, be thankful, because with some pruning to reduce its size it could become your garden's greatest asset. Yew grown as a tree will need diligent pruning to keep it manageable in size – but only once or twice a year. The upright Irish yew (*Taxus baccata* 'Fastigiata') is of great value for small gardens, though expensive to buy. Slow-growing and shade-tolerant, it keeps its columnar shape, making a year-round structural feature, with a crop of autumn berries to please the birds.

Salix exigua

Salix integra 'Hakuro-nishiki'

Syringa vulgaris 'Charles Joly'

Taxus baccata

Sorbus commixta 'Embley'

Sorbus 'Joseph Rock'

Sorbus aucuparia 'Sheerwater Seedling'

Sorbus
Rowans and whitebeams

Around 100 tree and shrub species belong to the genus *Sorbus*, and there are many more garden cultivars and hybrids. Almost all of them fall into one of two very different-looking and easily recognizable groups: rowans, with compound leaves and big bunches of conspicuous berries; and whitebeams, which have simple, oval leaves that are toothed at the edge and whitish on the underside. Both groups contain British native trees.

Rowans

Rowans make fine trees for smaller gardens. They are easy to grow, especially on light soils, and they need next to no maintenance or regular pruning. Most take up little lateral space, and their airy foliage casts only light shade. The berries are usually abundant, ripening early and differing according to variety; and all make a colourful impact from late summer and into autumn. They last until they are discovered by hungry birds, which tend to eat the red berries first and can soon strip a tree, especially in very cold weather.

Rowans with red and gold berries

Sorbus aucuparia is the native rowan or mountain ash. It grows wild in the most exposed and inhospitable places, brightening windswept moorlands and mountains with its berry crop. It is just as tough and beautiful in town gardens and streets, being more resistant to the effects of pollution than some other trees. Two upright, narrow cultivars that are particularly well adapted to smaller plots are 'Sheerwater Seedling' and 'Streetwise'. 'Aspleniifolia', another cultivar that is slender in shape, has daintily divided, fern-like foliage that makes an especially light canopy. You may encounter *Sorbus* 'Chinese Lace', whose finely divided foliage becomes an autumn palette of purples and reds to accompany the scarlet berries.

Sorbus 'Joseph Rock' has become very popular for its reliably large crop of golden berries – excellent for giving the illusion of sunshine on dull days or for brightening a dim corner. A seedling from 'Joseph Rock' is sold as *Sorbus* 'Autumn Spire', a narrow tree little more than 1m (40in) wide, but otherwise similar.

The popular *Sorbus commixta* 'Embley' has the edge over most rowans for reliable autumn colour, providing a double helping of flamboyance with its orange-red berries and fiery crimson foliage at the same time. The newer cultivar *Sorbus commixta* 'Olympic Flame' is similar but more upright in shape, with leaves that are bronze in spring. These change through green in summer to end the season orange-red and, like 'Embley', joining forces with the berries in a dual explosion of autumn colour.

Rowans with pink and white berries

A group of rowans from China and the Himalayas includes several rather refined, pretty garden trees. *Sorbus hupehensis*, always admired for its delicate, subtle bluish-green leaves, has more recently been joined by cultivars 'Pink Pagoda' and (more upright in shape) *Sorbus* 'Pink-Ness', which fruit even more abundantly than the species. Their bunches of coral-coloured berries form a pleasing contrast with the glaucous foliage and continue to make the tree an uplifting early-winter feature after leaf fall, eventually fading to white. Similar in foliage colour, though less reliable for autumn tints, is *Sorbus cashmiriana*. It has big bunches of large, white berries on red stalks, but makes a smaller, more shrub-like plant than *Sorbus hupehensis* and is also more drought-tolerant. Its flowers, opening from pinkish buds, are a cleaner white than those of many rowans. It likes a sheltered spot with light shade. *Sorbus vilmorinii*, another petite species, needs soil that does not dry out in summer. Its delicate foliage stays pretty throughout the growing season and well into autumn, when it turns a deep-crimson shade as the berries gradually change through shades of pink to white. 'White Wax' aptly describes the berries of a cultivar derived from *Sorbus koehneana*, a very compact, shrub-like rowan. It usually grows with several stems, and works well in a container.

Whitebeams

No sorbus grows very large, but whitebeams tend to make slightly bigger trees than rowans and, with heavier foliage, have a more solid presence – though they could never be described as oppressive. There are far fewer kinds of whitebeam than there are of rowans, and most of the whitebeams seen in gardens are the familiar *Sorbus aria* 'Lutescens'. This tree has its best moment in mid-spring, when each upright bud expands into a deep wineglass shape like a tulip or an opening magnolia bud. The downy, silvery-white undersides of the young leaves catch the light and shine in low sunlight – especially dramatic where the tree is seen against a dark background such as an evergreen tree or hedge, a tall brick wall, or a black weather-boarded garage or shed. (It can look distinctly less attractive later in the season, when the leaves sometimes begin to go brown and fall off long before autumn, usually as a result of scab disease.) The tree also produces white flowers, which can pass almost unnoticed against the silver leaves. *Sorbus aria* 'Majestica' (formerly 'Decaisneana') is a similar cultivar to 'Lutescens' but with larger leaves and fruits of a brighter red. You may also encounter the Swedish whitebeam, *Sorbus intermedia*, another similar tree with lobed leaves that are shiny and darker green on top.

Planting with rowans and whitebeams

The two types of *Sorbus* have quite different uses in planting schemes. The whitebeams' silvery leaves complement spring blues, whites and pastel colours. Rowans have a light canopy, so plants growing beneath are only lightly shaded; this makes them useful for any border – provided the berries are the right colour!

Sorbus hupehensis

Sorbus cashmiriana

Sorbus aria 'Lutescens'

Sorbus intermedia

Index

Page numbers in *italics* refer to trees in the Recommended small trees directory.

Acknowledgements

BBC Books and OutHouse would like to thank the following for their assistance in preparing this book: Andy McIndoe for advice and guidance; Robin Whitecross for picture research; Ruth Baldwin for proofreading; June Wilkins for the index.

Picture credits

Key t = top, b = bottom, l = left, r = right, c = centre

PHOTOGRAPHS

All photographs by Jonathan Buckley except those listed below.

GAP Photos Maxine Adcock 26b, 89a; Thomas Alamy 25(1) & 25br, 70b; Dave Bevan 5l, 19(1); Richard Bloom 23bl, 26f, 54c, 71d, 79c, 91a; Christina Bollen 18t, 27e, 81b; Elke Borkowski 2/3, 13t, 28, 32b, 84a; Julia Boulton 54t; Christa Brand 12; Nicola Browne 32t; Julie Danseraus 5r; Paul Debois 15(3); Carole Drake 31, 76c; Heather Edwards 33(1), 53(3); Ron Evans 79d; FhF Greenmedia 48(2), 54a, 73a, 74d; Tim Gainey 24; John Glover 26d, 62, 68, 70c, 71b; Virginia Grey 71; Jerry Harpur 46; Marcus Harpur 74c, 83a, 85a, 86c, 91c; Neil Holmes 64; Martin Hughes-Jones 16b, 20l, 54d, 77a, 80c, 84d, 88a & d, 89c; Jason Ingram 43b; Lynn Keddie 63; Geoff Kidd 66b; Fiona Lea 77b, 78b; Jenny Lilly 69c; Gerald Majumdar 27h, 72c; Sharon Pearson 21l, 78d, 90c; Howard Rice 13b, 48(1), 83b, 84b; S&O 65, 91b; JS Sira 4, 69a; Jason Smalley 66t; Friedrich Strauss 33l & (2), 48t; Graham Strong 15(2), 43t; Pat Tuson 61; Juliette Wade 70a; Jo Whitworth 76a; Rob Whitworth 21r, 53(2), 80d, 85d, 91d; Steven Wooster 25(3), 76b; Dave Zubraski 53(1)

Garden Collection FLPA 19(2); Modeste Herwig 42; Derek St Romaine 11; Nicola Stocken Tomkins 41

Garden Picture Library/Getty Images Mark Bolton 27g; Ron Evans 37l; Hemant Jariwala 87c; Andrea Jones 27f; Georgianna Lane 26c, 77c; Joshua McCullough 15(1); Mayer/Le Scanff 35; Howard Rice 27c, 37r; Didier Willery 69d

Garden World Images N+R Colborn 21c; Steffen Hauser 86a; Martin Hughes-Jones 34; Jonathan Need 90a; Trevor Sims 9, 27a, 90b; Lindsey Stock 85c

Sue Gordon 54b

Andrew McIndoe 22r, 26a, 69b, 74b, 75a & b, 76d, 79b, 81a & c, 83d, 84c, 85b, 88c, 89b

Marianne Majerus Garden Images 67

ILLUSTRATIONS

Julia Cady 29, 30

Lizzie Harper 14, 47, 50, 51, 55, 56 a, b, c & d, 57 a, b, d & e, 58b & d, 59a & c

Sue Hillier 56e, 57c, 58 a,c & e, 59b

Janet Tanner 10, 45, 49

Thanks are also due to the following designers and owners whose gardens appear in the book:

Beth Chatto, Beth Chatto Gardens, Essex 38; Anthony Goff, Spencer Road, London 36; John Massey, Ashwood Nurseries, Staffordshire 10; Ross Palmer 32t; RHS Wisley 5r; Joe Swift and Sam Joyce for The Plant Room 17; Helen Yemm, Eldenhurst, East Sussex 16